INNER CHILD HEALING JOURNAL AND WORKBOOK

2 in 1 | A Transformative Journey with Guided Exercises to Heal Emotional Wounds & Trauma, Build Unshakable Self-Esteem, and Achieve Lasting Inner Peace

Scarlett Kent

© Copyright 2024 Scarlett Kent

TABLE OF CONTENTS

INTRODUCTION

Welcome to this transformative journey of healing and self-discovery. This book has been created to guide you through a deep and personal process, combining the introspective nature of the Journal with the practical exercises of the Workbook. Together, these two parts will lead you toward healing past emotional wounds, building unshakable self-esteem, and finding lasting inner peace.

Why heal the inner child?

Your inner child represents the part of you that experienced emotional events during your early years. The emotions, memories, and traumas from your childhood can unconsciously affect your relationships, self-esteem, and how you handle challenges in your adult life. Healing these wounds means creating a safe space for your inner child, allowing you to release old pain, develop emotional awareness, and build healthier, more genuine relationships.

How to use this book

This book is structured as a 2-in-1 journey, divided into two complementary sections:

1. The Journal: In the first part of the book, you'll find a series of guided reflections and journaling prompts designed to help you explore your memories, emotions, and childhood experiences. It is a safe space where you can put your deepest thoughts into words, reconnecting with your inner child. This section will help you recognize emotional patterns and gain clarity on the true meaning behind your current reactions.

2. The Workbook: The second part is focused on practical exercises. Using techniques such as Cognitive Behavioral Therapy (CBT) and Shadow Work, the Workbook will guide you through a more structured healing process. Here, you will put into action

what you've discovered through the Journal, with exercises to challenge limiting beliefs, build self-esteem, and set stronger emotional boundaries.

What is the best way to approach this?

How you choose to use this book is entirely up to you, but here's a recommended path to get the most out of the experience:

1. Start with the Journal: Dedicate time to personal reflection. Complete the prompts and journaling exercises in the first part. This will help you reconnect with your inner child and understand the wounds from the past.
2. Move on to the Workbook: Once you feel that you've gained enough awareness, start the Workbook. The exercises will help you turn reflection into concrete action, using practical tools for healing and growth.
3. Alternate if Needed: If you prefer, you can alternate between the two sections, completing a journal prompt followed by a workbook exercise. This integrated approach allows you to balance reflection and action.

What can you expect?

Every person heals at their own pace, and this book is designed to let you move forward at your own rhythm. Working on your inner child can be challenging, but it is also incredibly rewarding. By the end of this journey, you will:

- Heal the emotional wounds from your past
- Build a solid, lasting self-esteem
- Cultivate inner peace and emotional stability
- Establish healthier, stronger relationships with others

This book is your guide, your companion on this journey. There is no right or wrong way to use it, only the path that is right for you. Take your time, allow yourself the freedom to reflect and grow, and let this journey lead you toward a more authentic, self-aware version of yourself.

Ready to begin? Open your Journal, start exploring your emotions, and use the Workbook to turn your reflections into healing actions.

THE BENEFITS OF INNER CHILD HEALING

Enhance relationships

Heal emotional wounds

Find inner peace

Reconnect with joy

Build self-compassion

Release past trauma

Boost self-esteem

MEDITATION AND RELAXATION EXERCISE

Before you begin your self-discovery journey through the pages of this book, let's lay the groundwork for a foundational practice that will serve as a centering and grounding ritual. This meditation and relaxation exercise will be your haven — a place to re-establish a connection with yourself, find serenity among the chaos of daily life, and prepare your mind and heart for the life-changing journey ahead.

Meditation for relaxation

Stress can be managed and reduced with relaxation meditation, which usually entails cultivating calm through an object of focus, such as your breath or a visualization. And we have proof that this is really effective! According to a study, people who used Headspace (a popular app for guided meditation) for just ten days saw an 11% reduction in stress, and those who used it for 30 days saw a 32% decrease in stress. Regular exercise allows our bodies to be more easily trained to find balance or the sweet spot between focus and relaxation.

So, how do you meditate for relaxation since not all meditation techniques are designed with that purpose in mind? Try this practice to help calm your body and mind: it involves deep breathing, body scanning, and awareness.

1. Pay attention to your breathing. Find a peaceful area and settle in. Take five long breaths in through your nose and out through your mouth to start. Imagine breathing in fresh air as you inhale and letting go of any stress in your body and mind as you exhale. Gently close your eyes after your fifth breath.

2. Check in. Take a minute to relax and feel comfortable in your skin. Become aware of your surroundings by observing sounds, tastes, scents, and your body weight on the chair or anywhere you're seated.

3. Body scan. Take note of any sore spots or regions of tension as you scan your whole body. Repeat the scan, noting the areas of the body that feel at ease. Set aside about twenty minutes for each scan. Just be aware of your thoughts as they arise; don't try to alter them, take note of your underlying feelings and observe them objectively.

4. Focus on your breath again. Return your attention to the act of breathing. As you focus on the feeling of your body rising and falling, breathe normally. Pay attention to how each breath feels. Is it shallow? Deep? Is it short or long? Quick or slow? Starting now, count the breaths silently as you inhale, exhale, and then inhale again, counting to ten. Then start again from one. You shouldn't worry if your thoughts stray. Simply return to focus on the breath.

5. Sit still. After your breathwork, sit quietly for 20 to 30 seconds and let your thoughts be free. It makes no difference if you are Zen and concentrated or racing through thoughts. Just follow the flow of your thoughts.

6. Get ready to wrap up. Lastly, return your focus to any bodily sensations you may be having. Consider your posture and the angle at which your feet touch the floor. Take note of any noises. Now, gradually open your eyes.

Pay attention to how your mind is feeling and then resolve to maintain that state of ease and relaxation for the rest of the day.

Reflection Prompt:

After finishing this meditation, Give some thought to these questions:

- After meditating, how does your physical self-perception change?
- What feelings or thoughts came to your mind during the exercise?
- Were there any difficult or comfortable times during the exercise?

This meditation practice is your anchor: you should return to it whenever you need self-connection and quiet.

Exercise: Who am I?

Answer questions to analyze and increase self-awareness:

- What is your name and how old are you?

_____

- How do you spend your spare time?

_____

- What activities bring you joy and allow your authentic self to shine?

_____

- Can you describe three words that you would use to define yourself?

_____

- In what ways do you consider yourself good, and what are you great at?

_____

- What do you love about your abilities?

_____

- Is there something specific you aspire to achieve someday?

_____

- Share one of your dreams and what it means to you.

_____

- If you could go on a trip with someone, who would that be? Where?

_____

- Who are the most important people in your life?

_____

- Name three things you've done that you are proud of.

_____

- How did you feel after accomplishing those proud moments?

_____

- How do you feel after completing daily essential tasks?

_____

- Do you believe that the tiniest victories matter in life? Why or why not?

_____

THE
INNER CHILD
HEALING
JOURNAL

Unlock Emotional Freedom and Self-Love through Guided Reflections, CBT Techniques, and Powerful Exercises to Heal Your Inner Child

Scarlett Kent

JOURNAL INTRODUCTION

The purpose of this journal is to support you as you work toward healing your inner child. Here are the main objectives of this guided journey:

- Self-reflection: through prompts and guided reflections, you will explore your memories, feelings, and experiences from childhood. This self-reflection aids in pinpointing the underlying reasons behind your present struggles.

- Emotional awareness: you will learn how to recognize and relate to your emotions. Developing a deeper comprehension of your emotions will enable you to face life's obstacles with greater calm and clarity.

- Healing childhood wounds: The exercises in this journal will help you confront and heal the wounds from your past. You will discover how to take care of your inner child and give yourself the love and support you require growing up.

- Overcoming emotional obstacles: you will learn how to get over emotional obstacles that have been impeding your personal growth. This involves confronting negative thoughts and swapping them out for ones that are empowering.

- Building self-love: this journal's main focus is on creating self-love. You will partake in activities that promote acceptance, self-care, and self-compassion.

- Integrating your authentic self in your life: lastly, this journal will help you integrate your inner child with your adult self. You can accept every part of who you are and live a more genuine life as a result of this integration.

How to use this journal

Using this journal is a flexible and personal process. To make the most of it, it's advisable to set aside time for journaling, making it a regular part of your day, whether daily, weekly, or at whatever interval works best for you, as consistency is key to making progress. It's important to establish a safe space, a peaceful, distraction-free area where you feel secure, allowing you to form a stronger connection with your inner child. Throughout this journey, be honest and open when responding to each prompt; there is no right or wrong answer, so feel free to express yourself as you see fit. Take your time, avoiding the rush to complete the exercises, and give yourself the necessary space to fully reflect and respond to each suggestion. Don't hesitate to use creative expressions, such as sketches, doodling, or other art forms, as sometimes words alone cannot fully convey what you feel. Practice self-compassion along the way, acknowledging your progress, no matter how small, as healing takes time. If certain memories or emotions become too overwhelming, don't hesitate to seek support from a therapist or a trusted friend; healing requires courage, and it's perfectly normal to ask for help.

What to Expect

This journal is structured to help you heal your inner child step by step. Below is a brief overview of what to expect: First, we will start by delving into the concept of the inner child and understanding the importance of healing through a brief overview of inner child work. You will then encounter guided reflections and prompts in each section designed to help you reflect on your childhood experiences, feelings, and habits. To combat negative thoughts and beliefs rooted in your early years, you will learn how to apply Cognitive Behavioral Therapy (CBT) techniques. Additionally, we will explore the hidden or repressed aspects of ourselves through shadow work, a process that brings these aspects to light and integrates them into your whole self. Throughout the journal, you will engage in self-acceptance, self-care, and self-love practices. Finally, to help you lead a more authentic and peaceful life, the last section of this book will focus on integrating your inner child with your adult self.

PART 1

UNDERSTANDING THE INNER CHILD

Imagine how your 6-year-old self would react if they saw you now. Would they give you an enthusiastic smile and a double high five? Reflecting on your younger self's perspective, would they be satisfied with the choices you've made, the path you've followed, and what you prioritize in life?

Becoming an adult

Everyone grows up at some point in their lives. We have to accept that we will eventually have to leave Neverland and enter the real world as adults. This happens fast, like a wind blast. It vanishes before we can discover its source. It doesn't take long for you to wake up and say, "I wish to return to my childhood; those were the best of times."

Our inner child never leaves our hearts and minds; it is a constant presence. Reestablishing a connection with our inner child may not be easy, but I assure you it's achievable if you dig deep enough. Do some soul-searching. There are moments when it's concealed beneath the weight of commitments, responsibilities, schedules, and aspirations for the future. We need to take a few deep breaths, quiet our racing minds, and embrace the wonders of childhood.

Reconnecting with childhood

Close your eyes and give it some time. Go back to your early childhood memories. You were carefree, daring, impulsive, and silly, and you relished the little things in life. You laughed and did imaginative things while lying outside. Stress did not yet exist, and all of these things came naturally. Having to eat veggies and have a bedtime may have been the biggest stressors in our lives.

Open your eyes, grab a notebook, and put down your impression of yourself. What about you did you find appealing? What brought you joy? What did you value most when you were a kid? Once you've written everything down, read it back to yourself. If you could go back in time and transform into the person you were at the age of eight, just think of what it would be like. What if there were more loving relationships, more playtime, more laughing, and more joyful moments in your life?

Your mission

Take initiative. Give it some more time, and choose three adjectives that best define you when you were a child. Make it your top goal to embody once again these words. Here are three adjectives that best sum up who I was when I was a kid: wild, loving, and open-minded. I acknowledge the existence of these three things within me. These are qualities that were formerly easily and completely attained.

We can still be happy as adults by changing our viewpoints and making moral choices without losing our childhood happiness. We must never forget to accept and love ourselves for who we are without passing judgment on anyone else or ourselves. Our pursuits should be directed toward the aspects of life that truly make us happy on the inside. We need to play outside, meet new people, and give hugs — plenty and lots of hugs.

GUIDED REFLECTIONS ON CHILDHOOD MEMORIES

If you want to begin identifying your inner child, you must think back on your childhood memories. These reflections will help you uncover the emotions and events that have molded your inner child. Here are some guided reflections to get you started:

Reflect on your earliest memories. Go back to your earliest memories. What catches your attention? These could be a moment of joy, fear, love, or sadness. Make an effort to recollect these memories in as much detail as you can. Where were you? Who was with you? How did you feel at the time?

Let's say that your first memory is from a birthday celebration. You still get goosebumps from seeing an exquisitely adorned cake and the comforting sound of your loved ones singing "Happy Birthday" to you. You also remember feeling a little let down when the toy you had been hoping for didn't arrive. This memory contains important aspects of your inner child's experiences, such as happiness and unfulfilled aspirations.

Identify significant people. Think back to the individuals who shaped your childhood, including your parents, siblings, grandparents, teachers, and friends. Reflect on the ways in which these people impacted you. What lessons about the world and yourself did they teach to you?

You may have felt confident and appreciated if your father often complimented your achievements. However, if a teacher consistently gives you negative feedback on your work, you may have internalized emotions of inadequacy. These influential figures contribute to the formation of your inner child's self-image.

Recall moments of joy and play. Think about the occasions in which you felt truly content and liberated. What activities did you enjoy? How did you show off your creativity and curiosity? These are the essential moments to realize the good things in your inner child.

Perhaps you loved drawing and spent hours creating colorful pictures. The creativity and passion of your inner child are evident in these memories. Remembering these joyful times can help you reconnect with these positive traits.

Acknowledge painful experiences. It's also critical to consider the difficult or painful experiences you had as a child. These could include moments of loneliness, depression, or fear. Healing requires acknowledging these memories, even if it can be challenging.

If you have memories of being lonely and insecure as a child, it may be because you moved about a lot and found it difficult to make friends. The first step in healing from these traumatic experiences is acknowledging them.

Reflect on unmet needs. Think about any desires you haven't satisfied growing up. These could be physical, like the desire for safety and stability, or emotional, like the need for love and acceptance. Finding these unfulfilled desires aids in determining the underlying traumas of your inner child.

If your parents were often absent because of their jobs, you may have felt neglected and unsupported emotionally. Your inner child's experience includes, among other things, this unfulfilled need for affection and parental presence.

EXERCISES TO RECOGNIZE THE INNER CHILD'S EMOTIONS AND THOUGHTS

Once you've reflected on your childhood memories, recognizing your inner child's emotions and thoughts comes next. Here are some exercises to help you connect with these aspects:

Emotion journaling. Make time every day to write about your emotions in your journal. Write down your current feelings first, and then reflect on how they might relate to the experiences of your inner child.

For instance, if you're nervous about a job presentation, think about similar feelings from your childhood. Have you ever had anxiety before presenting to a class? What feelings were you experiencing in that moment? Understanding the emotional terrain of your inner child can be achieved by making connections between your present feelings and previous encounters.

1._____   2._____   3._____

_____

_____

_____

Inner child dialogue. Write (or have a mental dialogue) with your inner child. Find out what they need and how they are feeling. Pay attention to their answers with kindness and understanding.

For instance, you might ask, "What's making you feel sad today?" and your inner child might respond, "I feel like no one cares about me." By having this conversation with yourself, you can learn a lot about the inner child's hidden emotions and thoughts.

_____

_____

_____

_____

_____

Body scan meditation. Try a body scan meditation to connect with the body sensations associated with your inner child's emotions. Take note of any places on your body that feel tight or uncomfortable, starting at the top of your head and working your way down to your toes.

For instance, when you focus on a particular memory during the body scan, you may feel a tightness in your chest. This physical sensation is a window into the feelings of your inner child. Recognize the feeling and reflect on what it might be trying to teach you about the emotions of your inner child.

_____

_____

_____

_____

_____

Sketching your inner child. Make a collage or drawing that embodies your inner child. You can visually express your inner child's emotions and thoughts with this exercise. You don't need to be an artist — just let your creativity flow.

For example, you could sketch an image of yourself when you were younger, surrounded by symbols representing your emotions and experiences, like a blazing sun for happiness or a broken heart for sadness. This visual representation helps you connect with your inner child in a tangible way.

Memory exploration. Pick a particular childhood memory and describe it deeply. Write down your thoughts, feelings, and details of what happened. After that, reflect on how this memory influences you now.

For instance, write down a detailed account of a bullying episode you experienced in school. How did you feel about it? What kind of thoughts crossed your mind? Reflect on how your interactions with others and sense of self-worth are affected by this event.

_____

_____

_____

_____

_____

_____

_____

Emotional self-check. Throughout the day, set aside some time to reflect on your emotions. Ask yourself, "How am I feeling right now? and why?" and "What might my inner child be experiencing?". This technique helps you stay connected with your inner child's emotions.

For example, take a moment to check in with your inner child if you're feeling overwhelmed during a hectic day. You may come to understand that your inner child is afraid and in need of comfort. It enables you to respond compassionately when you acknowledge these emotions.

_____

_____

_____

_____

_____

Visualization exercise. Close your eyes and picture a joyful, safe space where your inner child is at ease. This is where you can interact with your inner child and offer consolation and encouragement.

For instance, picture a lovely garden where your inner child is free to play and explore. Picture yourself having a conversation with your inner child while offering words of comfort and reassurance. By using this visualization, you can provide your inner child a safe haven.

Affirmations for the inner child. Create affirmations that specifically address your inner child's wants and feelings. Every day, repeat these affirmations to strengthen positive emotions and thoughts.

For instance, positive statements such as "You are safe," "You are loved," and "You are enough" will help dispel any negative thoughts that may be harbored by your inner child. Reprogramming your inner child's thoughts and emotions can be accomplished by repeating these affirmations.

_____   _____

_____   _____

_____   _____

Finding and connecting with your inner child is a deep and life-changing experience. Through introspection on your childhood and acknowledging the emotions and thoughts of your inner child, you can start to heal past wounds and grow in self-awareness and self-love.

EXPLORING CHILDHOOD WOUNDS

Examining your childhood traumas is one of the best ways to build your own resilience. Some people find that adulthood doesn't seem, sound, or feel fulfilling. They often question why their lives are such a horrible mess. That used to be the case for me until I realized that some of my inappropriate adult behaviors had their roots in my childhood. Our childhood trauma offers many answers to our adult struggles. Many individuals wonder, "Why must I return to those awful, emotional childhood memories? What relevance does my inner child have to my current life?".

Many also wonder, "Why didn't the therapist just say a few words and everything goes away?". Thankfully, some choose to remain active and take the time to look into, clean, and go through their old haunted closets.

Who and what is in the closet from your past?

The majority of our childhood wounds, including the traumatic ones, rarely heal or are even acknowledged by our parents or other important figures.

When you forgive the past before you've had a chance to deal with it fully, you end up taking responsibility for everything that has occurred to you. You can't even come close to achieving your goals when you're beating yourself up.

It serves no purpose to hold our parents responsible for their ignorance, carelessness, or what they abusively did. However, we might blame them for not providing us with the resources we need to grow into wholeness and peace. The good news is that we can now take responsibility for our lives as adults. Being aware enables us to use our freedom and power responsibly.

The Blame Game

Many of us were spoon-fed messages as kids that weren't good for our mental or emotional well-being. Even as we grew older, we continued to act according to outdated, harmful, and often unconscious behavioral habits, deeply rooted in our routines.

We feel more in charge of our destiny when we take responsibility for the scars we received as children. We blamed ourselves a lot and told ourselves things like, "If only I was smarter, prettier, kinder...they would see me as lovable and capable."

A small percentage of people are programmed in the other way. People attribute their discomfort to others: "If only they agreed with me and were more kind and smart."

Additionally, our emotions as children — sadness, fear, anger, and happiness —served as a guide. But we were taught to keep them in small, closed boxes with outdated directives from parents and other authority figures. When we lack a full emotional repertoire, we teach ourselves who we should be instead of really experiencing who we are.

Why explore your childhood wounds?

Finding out what thoughts, beliefs, and behaviors you hold from your childhood can help you with the following:

- Learn about the consequences of childhood trauma in later life.
- Change from a state of reflexive response to a deliberate form of action.
- Reveal your innermost feelings.
- Make your values clear.
- Keep your desired adult choices separated from the decisions you had to make as a child.
- Decide on the kind of partner, friend, coworker, parent, and individual you wish to be.
- Set yourself apart from your starting point and grow as a person.
- Lead a happier, more creative, and authentic life.

As Oprah Winfrey put it,

"One of life's greatest and most worthwhile undertakings is healing the wounds of the past. Understanding how and when you were programmed is crucial. As a result, you can change programs. It is your duty to do this. Not anyone else's.

The universe is governed by a single, unchangeable law. Each of us is in charge of our own existence. Relying on someone else to fulfill your happiness is a waste of time. You need to be brave enough to give yourself the love you didn't get."

TRAUMAS, ABANDONMENT, AND ABUSE

Welcome to the next phase of your healing. Here, we shall discuss childhood traumas, such as abuse, abandonment, and trauma. It's crucial to approach this next step with self-compassion and kindness. These exercises are intended to help you identify and understand these wounds so that you can start the healing process.

1. Traumas: describe a traumatic event from your childhood. What transpired, and how did you feel? How does this event continue to affect you today?

Reflect on traumatic events:

Think about the traumatic events from your childhood. What specific events stand out to you?

- _____
- _____
- _____
- _____

How did they make you feel at the time?

_____
_____
_____
_____

How do they make you feel now?

_____

_____

_____

_____

Emotional impact:

How did these events impact your emotions and behaviors?

_____

_____

_____

_____

Did you develop any coping mechanisms to deal with the trauma?

_____

_____

_____

_____

Physical sensations:

Do you have any physical reactions in your body as you recall these incidents?

_____

_____

_____

_____

Where do you feel tension or discomfort?

_____

_____

_____

_____

Triggers:

Are there certain circumstances, individuals, or locations that bring up recollections of these traumatic experiences?

_____

_____

_____

_____

How do you typically respond to these triggers?

_____

_____

_____

_____

2. Abandonment: think about a time when you felt abandoned or neglected as a child. Who was part of it, and what were the surrounding circumstances? What views about other people and yourself have you changed as a result of this experience?

Feelings of abandonment:

Reflect on moments when you felt abandoned or neglected. Who was involved?

_____

_____

_____

_____

What were the circumstances?

_____

_____

_____

_____

Emotional response:

How did the feelings of abandonment impact your sense of self-worth and security?

_____

_____

_____

_____

Did you feel unworthy of love or attention?

_____

_____

_____

_____

Patterns of abandonment:

Are there recurring patterns of abandonment in your relationships?

_____

_____

_____

_____

How do these patterns affect your current relationships and interactions with others?

_____

_____

_____

_____

Coping mechanisms:

How did you cope with feelings of abandonment as a child?

_____

_____

_____

_____

Do you still use these coping mechanisms today?

_____

_____

_____

_____

3. Abuse: write about an instance of abuse you experienced as a child. Who was involved, and what happened? How has this experience influenced your feelings about yourself and your relationships?

Types of abuse:

Identify the types of abuse you experienced (physical, emotional, etc.).

_____

_____

_____

_____

Who was the abuser, and what was the nature of the abuse?

_____

_____

_____

_____

Immediate feelings:

How did you feel immediately after the abusive incidents?

_____

_____

_____

_____

Did you feel fear, shame, guilt, or anger?

_____

_____

_____

_____

Long-term impact:

How has the abuse affected your long-term emotional and mental health?

_____

_____

_____

_____

Do you struggle with trust, self-esteem, or anxiety as a result?

_____

_____

_____

_____

Seeking help:

Have you ever sought help or support for dealing with the abuse? If not, what has prevented you from doing so?

_____

_____

_____

_____

PERSONAL EXPERIENCES

Take some time to reflect on your responses to the questions and prompts. Use the space below to write about your personal experiences. Remember, this is your safe space to express yourself openly and honestly.

Write about your experiences with trauma, abandonment, or abuse. Describe your feelings, thoughts, and any physical sensations you notice. Reflect on how these experiences have impacted your life and what you need to heal.

Date: ....

Topic: Exploring childhood wounds

_____

_____

_____

_____

_____

_____

_____

_____

_____

_____

_____

_____

_____

_____

_____

_____

_____

_____

_____

_____

_____

_____

_____

PART 2

HEALING TECHNIQUES

People often carry painful childhood memories into adulthood. Childhood trauma often resurfaces as problems in adult relationships, especially sexual and parent-child relationships, though friendships and the workplace can also become difficult spots. We often replicate many of the same behavioral patterns from our childhood when these maladaptive behavior patterns appear in our adult relationships. When our neglected and wounded inner child comes out as an adult, we respond impulsively and selfishly, get into messy relationships, and use unhealthy coping mechanisms like drugs, alcohol, and binge eating to deal with stress.

Many adults show infantile behavior in response to emotional distress or feelings of threat. This could manifest as storming out of a conversation, stonewalling or refusing to speak, stomping feet, slamming doors during an argument, or any combination of these.

Accepting your inner child and realizing that healing can start with a curiosity about what happened and a reconnection with your emotions are both vital and helpful.

Before starting the healing process with your inner child, first it's important to recognize that this work will take time. There is no quick fix to the pain associated with childhood trauma or distress. Inner child work is essentially an ongoing, mindful dialogue between the inner child and the adult self.

CBT FOR INNER CHILD HEALING

Cognitive Behavioral Therapy, or CBT, is an effective tool for changing negative thoughts and beliefs that result from childhood events. If you can identify and change these negative beliefs, you can tend to and heal your inner child. Here are several CBT exercises to aid in this process, along with sheets for recording your thoughts and feelings.

CBT exercises to identify and change negative thoughts

1. Thought monitoring

Objective: To become conscious of your negative thoughts and how they affect your feelings, actions, and thinking.

Instructions: Pay attention to your thoughts throughout the day, especially in circumstances that trigger strong emotions. When unpleasant thoughts come to mind, write them down and note the context. For instance, write down any thoughts you have that make you feel inadequate, such as "I'm not good enough," along with the circumstances that made them come to mind (e.g., getting ready for a work presentation).

Thought monitoring sheet

Date	Situation	Negative Thoughts	Emotions felt	Intensity
[Date]	[Describe the situation]	[Write the negative thought]	[Describe the emotion(s)]	[Rate 1-10 intensity]

2. Thought challenging

Objective: To contest and dispute the veracity of negative thinking.

Instructions: Consider asking yourself the following questions for each negative thought you've identified:

- Is this thought based on assumptions or facts?
- What proof do I use to back up my thoughts?
- What evidence do I have against this thought?
- Is there another, more impartial way to look at this?

For instance, you can confront the thought that "I'm not good enough" by pointing out your achievements in the past and the encouraging comments you've had, which disprove this negative notion.

Thought challenging sheet

Date	Negative Thought	Evidence For	Evidence Against	Balanced Thought
[Date]	[Write the negative thought]	[List evidence supporting the thought]	[List evidence contradicting the thought]	[Write the balanced thought]

3. Cognitive restructuring

Objective: To replace negative thoughts with more practical and happy ones.

Instructions: After challenging a negative thought, formulate a kinder one instead. Think only positive, encouraging, and realistic thoughts. For example, swap out "I'm not good enough" with "I've prepared well for this presentation, and I can do a good job."

Cognitive reconstructing sheet

Date	Negative Thought	Challenged Thought	New Balanced Thought	Emotions felt	Intensity
[Date]	[Write the negative thought]	[Write the challenged thought]	[Write the new balanced thought]	[Describe the emotions]	[Rate 1-10 intensity]

4. Behavioral experiments

Objective: To evaluate the validity of negative thoughts using real-life experiments.

Instructions: Choose a negative thought and create a little experiment to see how accurate it is. Examine the outcomes and consider how they confirm or contradict the negative thought. For instance, if you think "people will judge me if I speak up in meetings," test this by bringing up a minor point during a meeting and seeing how other people respond.

Behavioral experiment sheet

Date	Negative Thought	Experiment	Prediction	Actual Outcome	Reflection
[Date]	[Write the negative thought]	[Describe the experiment]	[What do you think will happen?]	[What happened?]	[Reflect on the outcome and what you learned]

5. Thought replacement

Objective: To consciously replace negative thoughts with positive affirmations.

Instructions: Find a negative thought that keeps coming up and make an affirmation that will help you stop it. Regularly repeat this affirmation, especially when the negative thought comes up. For instance, change "I'm not lovable" to "I am worthy of love and respect" and repeat this affirmation every day.

Thought Replacement Sheet

Date	Negative Thought	Positive Affirmation	Context/Situation	Emotions felt
[Date]	[Write the negative thought]	[Write the positive affirmation]	[Describe the context/situation]	[Describe the emotions]

6. Gratitude Practice

Objective: Shifting attention from unpleasant thoughts to positive parts of life.

Instructions: Write down three things for which you are thankful every day. Think about the feelings you get from these positive aspects. For example, "I'm grateful for my creativity, my health, and my supportive friends."

Gratitude Practice Sheet

Date	Gratitude Entry 1	Gratitude Entry 2	Gratitude Entry 3
[Date]	[Write the first gratitude entry]	[Write the second gratitude entry]	[Write the third gratitude entry]

SHADOW WORK FOR INNER CHILD HEALING

Shadow work is a transformative process that entails facing and integrating your hidden parts, the aspects of yourself that you tend to ignore or cover up because you think they are undesirable or bad. By shedding light on these shadow parts, you can become whole, healed, and self-aware. Let's explore how you can confront and integrate your shadow, along with some journaling exercises to help you explore it.

Confronting and integrating hidden parts of yourself

Let's first clarify what the shadow is. The shadow is the unconscious part of your personality, made up of all the traits and behaviors you have suppressed or denied. These shadows are shaped by past experiences, particularly during childhood, in which particular behaviors or emotions were judged inappropriate by classmates, caretakers, or society at large. Integrating your shadow leads to better relationships, emotional well-being, and increased self-awareness.

Start by identifying your shadow. Engaging in self-reflection is a smart place to start. Consider the qualities and actions you dislike in other people. These traits are often reflections of your own shadow. Observe any patterns in your behavior as well as any triggers that cause intense emotional responses. These can point to shadow aspects. Dreams should also be taken seriously since they may disclose hidden aspects of your psyche.

Instead of passing judgment when you face your shadow, approach it with kindness and curiosity. Acknowledge that certain aspects of yourself developed as coping mechanisms. Recognize that everyone has a shadow and that it is a sign of strength rather than weakness to own it. Have a conversation with yourself about your shadow. Find out what it needs and how it has tried to protect you.

Accepting your duality is essential to integrating your shadow. You should start to recognize that every trait has advantages and disadvantages. For example, transform negative traits into constructive ones: channel your anger, for instance, into assertive conversation. To remain conscious of your shadow and incorporate it into your everyday life, engage in mindfulness exercises. Remember that shadow work is an ongoing process. Regular reflection on what you do, your emotions and your thoughts will help you continue to integrate your shadow. Seeking guidance from a therapist or a reliable friend can be beneficial in managing challenging emotions and insights.

Journaling exercises to explore your personal shadow

Let's get started with some journaling activities that will enable you to examine your shadow.

Traits in others. Write down the traits you dislike most in others. Reflect on how you may possess these traits as well but to a lesser degree. For example, list three traits you dislike in others. How do these traits make you feel, and why do you think you react strongly to them?

_____

_____

_____

Inner dialogue. Engage in a written dialogue with your shadow. Ask it questions and write down the responses you imagine your shadow might give. For example, write a dialogue between you and your shadow. Ask your shadow what it needs, why it behaves the way it does, and how it has tried to protect you.

Questions	Answers

What did you learn from conversation?

_____

_____

_____

Positive traits. Identify traits you admire in others and reflect on how you might embody these traits. Often, these admired traits are underdeveloped aspects of yourself.

List three traits you admire in others.

1. _____
2. _____
3. _____

How do you develop these traits inside yourself?

_____

_____

_____

What steps can you take to develop these positive aspects?

_____

_____

_____

Transforming negative traits. Choose a negative trait you've identified in yourself and brainstorm ways to transform it into a positive action.

Select one negative trait you've identified in yourself.

- _____

How can you transform this trait into something positive? For example, if you tend to be overly critical, how can you use that critical eye to improve situations constructively?

_____

_____

_____

_____

_____

_____

SELF-COMPASSION AND SELF-LOVE

It's essential to cultivate self-love and self-compassion in order to heal your inner child. It's all about being nice, considerate, and supportive of yourself as you would a close friend. Here, we'll look at some self-compassion exercises, self-love reflection prompts, and writing a sincere letter to your inner child.

Exercises to develop self-compassion

Let's start with a self-compassion exercise. The first one we're going to try is the self-compassion break. This involves taking a moment in the middle of a stressful situation to acknowledge your suffering, that suffering is a normal human experience, and that you have to be kind to yourself. Here's how you can do it:

- **Acknowledge your suffering.** When you're going through a tough time, pause and say to yourself, "This is really hard right now."
- **Recognize shared humanity**. Remind yourself that suffering is a part of life. Say, "Everyone goes through challenges like this."
- **Be kind to yourself.** Offer yourself comforting words. Say, for instance: "May I treat myself with kindness in this moment. May I be compassionate to myself when I need it."

Another helpful technique is the loving-kindness meditation. This involves telling positive affirmations to yourself. In a peaceful moment, close your eyes, and tell yourself: "May I have a joyful life! May I live a healthy life! May I be safe! May I live comfortably!" Allow these words to settle into your heart as you repeat them slowly and with intention.

Prompts to reflect on self-love

Thinking about self-love can improve your relationship with yourself and help you realize how valuable you are. Here are some starter prompts to get you started.

First, consider a moment when you experienced genuine love and appreciation. What was the occasion, and how did you feel about it? Write down your thoughts while thinking about how you could experience that again.

_____

_____

_____

_____

_____

Write about the qualities you admire in yourself. What makes you unique? How have these qualities helped you in life? Celebrate these traits and acknowledge your strengths.

_____

_____

_____

_____

_____

Reflect on the way you talk to yourself. Is your inner dialogue kind and supportive, or is it critical and harsh? Write about how you can shift your inner voice to be more compassionate and loving.

_____

_____

_____

_____

_____

Letter to the inner child

Writing to your inner child can be a powerful way to express love, forgiveness, and understanding. It helps you create a connection with the younger version of yourself who may have experienced neglect, fear, or hurt. This is a guide to help you in writing the letter.

First, find a peaceful area away from distractions. Close your eyes and inhale deeply while visualizing your younger self in front of you. Picture them well and experience the emotions that come with them.

Begin your letter with a loving greeting. For example, "Dear [Your Name] at [Age], I see you, and I'm here for you." Acknowledge their feelings and experiences. Tell them it's acceptable to experience hurt, fear, or sadness. Say something like: "I know you've been through a lot, and I understand how hard it has been for you."

Next, offer encouraging and comforting words. Tell your inner child that they are loved, safe, and valued at this very moment. You might write: "You are so appreciated and loved, exactly as you are. It's not necessary to be perfect to deserve affection. I'm here to look out for and defend you."

Remind your inner child of their perseverance and strength by sharing some of your best moments or accomplishments. You might add: "Remember when you stood up for yourself at school? That took so much courage. You have always been strong and brave."

Lastly, say that you will always be available to your inner child. Tell them you will always love and be there for them. Use a heartfelt closure to wrap up your letter, like: "With all my love, [your Name], as an adult."

PART 3

CREATING A NEW NARRATIVE

As children, we were often powerless and dependent on the adults around us for emotional support. Time itself seemed to stretch endlessly, and due to our still-developing minds, we often took personal blame for problems that arose. Unfortunately, not all adults were adept at managing their emotions or ours. This neglect or mishandling of our emotional distress could reinforce feelings of invisibility, unease, and entrapment. In the absence of nurturing support, our natural responses to stress, fight, flight, freeze, or fawn could become our default reactions. As we grew, we might have suppressed our feelings to the extent our caregivers acknowledged them, accumulating an emotional backlog that risks erupting during stressful adult situations.

Examples of inner child narratives

"Inner child narratives" refer to the deep-seated stories we tell ourselves based on childhood experiences. These narratives can significantly influence our feelings of self-worth and our reactions to life's challenges, often perpetuating feelings of isolation, worthlessness, despair, and a sense of endless struggle. Here are some examples of such narratives:

- **Endlessness:** "It seems never-ending. Nothing will ever improve. I have no power."
- **Inadequacy:** "I'm never good at anything! Why am I acting this way? I am horrible."
- **Anxiety:** "Worse things could happen if I stop worrying!"
- **Neglect:** "No one is listening to me, even when I need help. Help!"
- **Hyper-vigilance:** "I have to stay vigilant at all times; it's not safe to relax."
- **Loneliness:** "I'm by myself once again. I'll be alone forever."
- **Dependency:** "To live, I must have a certain person's love." To get them to notice me, I will do anything."

Inner child narratives and associated emotions

The inner child narrative might likewise arouse strong emotions:

- All of a sudden, you feel terrified, confused, and like a young child.
- There's a feeling of panic, urgency, or desperation.
- Your behavior seems impulsive or reactive.
- You have a strong sense of helplessness, hopelessness, or abandonment.

Is your inner child narrative in action?

To start the process of healing your inner child, identify your inner child's narrative. Follow these steps to determine whether you are experiencing an inner child narrative:

- Take a moment to observe your emotions. Do you feel defeated and let down? Or agitated, impetuous, and reactive?
- Do you sense strong feelings? Are they oppressing you?
- How do you feel about the current situation?
- Be mindful of the words you use when speaking to yourself. Is there a narrative about giving up? Of finding yourself trapped? Abandoned? Scared? Sad? Lost?
- If so, pause for a moment and spend some time reconnecting with your inner child.

RECONCILIATION WITH THE PAST

Making peace with your past is essential to getting better and moving on. This process often involves forgiving yourself and others. Let's look at some exercises that can support your reconciliation and forgiveness. Additionally, we'll provide you space to write letters outlining your forgiving journey.

Exercises to forgive oneself and others

One of the most effective ways to break the grip that old hurts have on you is through forgiveness. It involves releasing yourself from the emotional load rather than forgetting or condoning what happened. Here are some exercises to help you forgive yourself and others.

1. Embrace your feelings

First, recognize your feelings. As you sit quietly, reflect on the feelings that come to mind when you remember the person or circumstance that caused you pain. Allow yourself to feel these emotions without judging them. Acknowledging your feelings is the first step towards letting them go.

2. Think about the effect

Think about the effects that anger and resentment have had on your life. Write down how these negative emotions have influenced your well-being, relationships, and overall happiness. This reflection can help you understand the importance of forgiveness.

3. Practice self-compassion

When it comes to forgiving yourself, self-compassion is key. Think about a mistake or regret that you struggle to forgive yourself for. Write yourself a compassionate letter, acknowledging that we all make mistakes and that you deserve forgiveness just as much as anyone else. Remember that you are only human and that obstacles are often what lead to personal development.

4. Taking a perspective

Consider the other person's perspective when evaluating the situation. What might have led them to act that way? This doesn't excuse their behavior but can help you understand it better, making it easier to let go of the hurt. Write down your thoughts and feelings during this exercise.

5. Letting go ritual

Create a letting go ritual. Put your list of things you need to let go of and forgive down on paper. Next, locate a quiet, secure area where you can burn the paper to represent the release of your hurt and anger. As you watch the paper burn, picture the negative emotions dissipating with the smoke.

6. Daily affirmations

Incorporate daily affirmations into your routine to reinforce forgiveness. Repeat phrases like: "I forgive myself for past mistakes" or "I release the hurt and embrace peace." These affirmations can help rewire your thinking and promote a forgiving mindset.

WRITING FORGIVENESS AND RECONCILIATION LETTERS

Writing letters of forgiveness can be a cathartic and transformative experience. Below, you'll find a guide for writing forgiveness and reconciliation letters to yourself and others, along with dedicated space to write these letters.

Forgiveness letter to yourself

Start by addressing yourself warmly, acknowledging the specific actions or behaviors you're seeking to forgive. Express understanding and compassion for the circumstances that led to those actions. Then, affirm your commitment to learning and growing from these experiences.

Dear [Your Name],

I know you've been carrying the weight of past mistakes and regrets. I understand the pain and guilt you've felt because of these experiences. But I want you to know that you did the best you could at the time with the knowledge and resources you had.

I forgive you for [specific actions or behaviors]. I recognize that these actions came from a place of hurt, confusion, or fear. You are human, and it's okay to make mistakes. What's important is that you've learned from these experiences and are committed to growing and healing.

From this moment on, I release the guilt and shame. I choose to embrace self-compassion and understanding. You deserve forgiveness and love, and I am here to give that to you.

With all my love and compassion,

[Your Name]

_____

_____

_____

_____

_____

_____

_____

_____

_____

_____

_____

_____

_____

_____

_____

_____

_____

_____

_____

Forgiveness letter to others

Address the person who hurt you, acknowledging the pain they caused. Express your feelings honestly, then convey your understanding or perspective on why they might have acted that way. Finally, state your intention to forgive them and let go of the negative emotions tied to the past.

Dear [Person's Name],

I want to acknowledge the pain and hurt caused by [specific actions or behaviors]. It has taken me time to process and understand the impact of these actions on my life. I felt [describe your emotions], and it has been a heavy burden to carry.

I've invested a lot of time in trying to understand why you might have acted the way you did. Although it doesn't justify what you did, I understand that everyone has different challenges and has different motivations for their actions. I choose to see you as a flawed human being, just like myself.

I'm going to choose to forgive you today. I let go of the bitterness and rage that had been holding me back. By forgiving you, I am able to let go of the hurt from the past. I'm ready to go on with a peaceful head and a lighter heart.

With understanding and compassion,

[Your Name]

_____

_____

_____

_____

_____

_____

_____

_____

_____

_____

_____

_____

_____

_____

_____

_____

_____

_____

Reconciliation letter to someone who hurt you to repair the relationship

If you feel ready to reach out and reconcile with someone who has hurt you, use this template to express your desire for healing and rebuilding the relationship. Acknowledge the hurt, share your feelings, and express your willingness to move forward together.

Dear [Person's Name],

I am writing to address the hurt caused by [specific actions or behaviors]. It has taken me time to understand and analyze my emotions in light of what transpired. I felt [describe your emotions], and it affected our relationship deeply.

Despite the pain, I value our relationship and the good times we've shared. I want us to move past this and find a way to heal together. I am open to understanding your perspective and working towards rebuilding trust.

I hope we can have an honest conversation about what happened and how we can support each other in moving forward. I am committed to forgiveness and reconciliation and hope you are willing to join me on this journey.

With hope and openness,

[Your Name]

_____

_____

_____

_____

_____

_____

_____

_____

_____

_____

_____

_____

_____

_____

_____

_____

_____

_____

_____

VISUALIZATION OF THE FUTURE

One of the most effective ways to focus on the life you desire is to visualize a future free from the traumas of the past. By practicing manifestation and visualization, you can clearly see your goals and take action to turn them into reality. Let's get started with some exercises to help you visualize and manifest your personal goals, as well as prompts to help you imagine a future free of past traumas.

Imagining a future free from past traumas

Find a peaceful, comfortable spot to relax and concentrate for a moment. Close your eyes, inhale deeply, and allow your thoughts to wander while you consider the following prompts.

1. Your ideal day. Imagine a day in your future when you feel completely free from the weight of past traumas.

What does this ideal day look like?

_____

_____

_____

_____

Describe your surroundings, the people you're with, and how you feel throughout the day.

_____

_____

_____

_____

What activities do you engage in?

_____

_____

_____

_____

How do you interact with others?

_____

_____

_____

_____

How do you end your day, feeling content and at peace?

_____

_____

_____

_____

2. Your future self. Visualize yourself a few years from now, having healed from past traumas.

How do you look?

_____

_____

_____

_____

How do you carry yourself?

_____

_____

_____

_____

What are some of the positive changes you notice in yourself?

_____

_____

_____

_____

Imagine your future self-talking to you today. What advice or encouragement would they offer?

_____

_____

_____

_____

3. Achieving your dreams. Think about a dream or goal that you've always wanted to achieve but felt held back by past traumas. Visualize yourself accomplishing this dream.

How do you feel in that moment of achievement?

_____

_____

_____

_____

What steps did you take to get there?

_____

_____

_____

_____

What support and resources did you have along the way?

_____

_____

_____

_____

4. Overcoming challenges. Picture a future where you encounter challenges, but you handle them with resilience and confidence.

What coping strategies do you use?

_____

_____

_____

_____

How do you maintain your emotional balance?

_____

_____

_____

_____

Visualize yourself overcoming these obstacles and growing stronger with each experience.

_____

_____

_____

_____

5. Positive relationships. Envision your future surrounded by positive, supportive relationships.

Who are the people present in your life?

_____

_____

_____

_____

How do they support and uplift you?

_____

_____

_____

_____

How do you nurture these relationships and contribute to their positivity?

_____

_____

_____

_____

VISUALIZATION AND MANIFESTATION EXERCISES FOR PERSONAL GOALS

After you have visualized a future free from past traumas, let's concentrate on exercises that will help you visualize and realize your personal goals. Through these exercises, you will develop a clear vision of your goals and take concrete measures toward realizing them.

Creating a vision board

A vision board is a way to put your aspirations and goals onto paper. Creating one will help you stay inspired and focused. Gather magazines, poster board, or large sheets of paper, scissors, and glue. Cut out pictures, phrases, and sentences from the magazines that resonate with your dreams and ambitions. Organize them on the board in a way that you find significant. Put your vision board in a spot where you'll see it daily, so it can serve as both a source of inspiration and a reminder of your goals.

Guided visualization exercise

Sit in a comfortable position and close your eyes. Breathe deeply many times, letting your body come to rest. Imagine a specific goal you wish to accomplish. Picture yourself making the necessary moves to accomplish it, advancing through each stage with self-assurance and determination. Finally, imagine the outcome and the sensation of reaching your goal. Spend a few minutes fully immersing yourself in this visualization, then open your eyes and write down any insights or action steps that came to mind.

Manifestation journaling

Journaling can help you achieve your goals. Put your goals down on paper in the present tense, as if you've already reached them. For instance, don't write "I want to stay healthy" instead, write "I am well, healthy, and full of energy." Be specific and detailed. Next, list the steps you need to take to achieve these goals. Divide them into doable tasks and give each one a deadline. Regularly review your journal to monitor your development and make the changes that are needed.

Affirmations for success

It's possible to rewire your mind for success by employing positive affirmations. Create a list of affirmations that will help you achieve your goals and say them aloud each day. For instance, if your goal is to boost your self-esteem, you may write: "I am confident and worthy of love and respect." Write these affirmations on sticky notes and stick them all over your house or office as a daily reminder of your aspirations.

Mindfulness meditation

Mindfulness meditation helps you stay present and goal-focused. Find a peaceful area, take a comfortable seat, and close your eyes. Become aware of your breathing and the sensation of air entering and leaving your body. When your mind wanders, bring them back to your breathing. Shift your focus to your goals after a short while. Visualize every goal as a mental seed that has been sown. Imagine that with your care and attention, these seeds will grow and bloom. Spend a few minutes nurturing these goals with your focused intention, then slowly open your eyes and return to the present moment.

Action planning

A clear plan of action is necessary to accomplish your goals. First, briefly state your main goal. Divide it into smaller, more doable tasks. Establish due dates and note any resources or assistance you may require for each phase. Make a schedule or to-do list to monitor your progress. Consistently review and modify your action plan as necessary to stay on course. It's time to bring it all together.

Time to bring everything together

Visualization and manifestation are about more than just dreaming — they involve actively shaping your future. By using these prompts and exercises, you can create a vivid picture of a life free from past traumas and take tangible steps toward achieving your personal goals. Keep in mind, the future you imagine is attainable. Stay optimistic, stay focused, and continue moving forward. You have the power to create the life you desire!

PART 4

PRACTICAL TOOLS AND DAILY EXERCISES

I wish I had known that I had a wounded inner child when I was younger. I was stuck with false beliefs about my own values, my place in the world, and my ability to trust other people that I had internalized as a child. I continued to have a variety of emotional problems as a result of feeling limited and stuck.

I was cut off from myself, love, wisdom, and my own guidance. After six years of studying psychology, I was told that my brain was hardwired. There remained, nevertheless, a spark of optimism and confidence in my possibility to recover.

That's when I began my spiritual journey to find healing and inner serenity. I didn't know that I could heal and provide my inner child the love and acceptance he required until I learned about inner child work. I spent years searching for the truth from other spiritual teachers by looking outside of me. However, I came to understand that I could be my own inner parent and provide myself with all the love I required rather than searching for a supernatural and occasionally terrifying parent-in-the-sky.

I had a strong sense that my inner child was a reflection of the child I used to be, and I was very self-aware, but I didn't know where to begin. People would tell me repeatedly that I needed to heal my inner child, but they were unable to provide me with guidance, so I decided to look for it on my own.

I've therefore spent the last few years trying to uncover the secrets of inner child healing.

Since then, I've discovered my own inner child healing techniques, which have been nothing short of a miracle in helping me to forgive myself and find peace. Inner child work, in my opinion, has been the most helpful thing I've done to integrate and heal from my past. It has enabled me to address unmet emotional needs from my early years and get to the root of the childhood traumas that were preventing me from moving forward in life.

Even if I'm still learning, inner child work has given me the greatest sense of calm, inner power, and love I've ever experienced. The fact that it's a self-healing tool that I have complete control over is what I love the most about it. Even though I can't go back in time, I've discovered my inner parent, who will provide me with the secure base my inner child needs.

These are some inner child exercises that, after trying a few different things, enabled me to connect with my inner child.

DAILY HEALING ROUTINE

Nurturing your inner child and promoting long-lasting personal growth requires you to establish a daily healing routine. Including self-care exercises in your daily schedule will help you stay balanced, centered, and emotionally aware. Let's explore some suggestions for daily self-care practices, and I'll provide sheets to record your daily progress.

1. Morning meditation

Spend a short while in meditation to begin your day. Find a quiet place, settle in, and pay attention to your breathing. This practice can help you center yourself and set a positive tone for the day. Visualize yourself enveloped in warmth and light during your meditation, bringing calm and positivity into you.

2. Journaling

Set aside some time every day to write in your journal. Make some notes about your experiences, reflect on your emotions and thoughts, and decide what you want to do that day. Journaling helps you better comprehend your inner world and process your feelings. Make use of opening phrases like "Today, I feel…" or "One thing for which I am thankful is…"

3. Workout

Take up a fun physical activity that you enjoy. Working out can help relieve stress and improve your mood, whether you're doing yoga, walking, dancing, or exercising. Make time for this activity every day for at least 20 to 30 minutes.

4. Mindful eating

Take a thoughtful approach to eating by giving your meals your whole attention. Eat mindfully — noticing the aromas and sensations — and take your time. By doing this, you can enhance your overall well-being and develop a healthier relationship with food.

5. Practice gratitude

Spend a few minutes each day remembering all of your blessings. You can do this by reflecting in silence or keeping a gratitude journal. Acknowledging your life's blessings can help you change your perspective and become more emotionally resilient.

6. Positive affirmations

Include the use of affirmations in your daily practice. Recite affirmations that speak to you on paper and throughout the day. Some that can help support a good self-image and increase confidence are, for example: "I am worthy of respect and love" and "I am capable of achieving my goals."

7. Creative expression

Take up a creative activity that makes you happy, like painting, crafting, music writing, or drawing. Using your creative expression to connect with your inner child and let go of pent-up emotions can be healing.

8. Evening reflection

Reflect for a moment as you wrap up your day. Consider your achievements, your setbacks, and the knowledge you gained. By doing this, you can analyze your experiences and be ready for a peaceful night's sleep. You may write down thoughts in your journal or just sit in silence for a short while.

DAILY HEALING ROUTINE SHEET

Date: _____

Morning Meditation

Duration: _____

Reflections:_____

_____

Journaling

Today's Thoughts and Emotions:

_____

_____

_____

Daily Intentions:

_____

_____

_____

Physical Activity

Type of Activity: _____

Duration: _____

Mindful Eating

Meals: _____

Reflections: _____

Gratitude Practice

Things I'm Grateful For: Reflections:

_____

_____

_____

Positive Affirmations

Affirmations for Today:

_____

_____

Creative Expression

Activity: _____

Duration: _____

Evening Reflection

What Went Well:

_____

Challenges Faced:

_____

_____

Lessons Learned:

_____

_____

WEEKLY REFLECTION EXERCISES

Reflecting on your progress and challenges every week is a crucial part of your healing journey. It allows you to keep track of what you've accomplished, understand the obstacles you've faced, and set new intentions for the coming week. These are some questions to get you to reflect on your obstacles and evaluate your progress.

1. What went well this week?

Think about the highlights of your week. What are the positive experiences or achievements you had? Reflect on moments when you felt happy, proud, or content. Write down these experiences to remind yourself of the progress you're making.

2. What challenges did I face?

Identify any difficulties or obstacles you encountered during the week. These might be related to your emotions, relationships, or daily routine. Give a detailed account of these difficulties, mentioning your reactions to them and how they influenced you.

3. How did I handle stress and difficult emotions?

Reflect on how you managed stress and difficult emotions. Did you use any coping strategies? Were they effective? Consider times when you experienced stress and how you handled those feelings. Jot down the techniques that worked for you or any areas you'd like to improve.

4. What did I learn about myself?

Consider any new insights or lessons you've learned about yourself this week. This might have to do with how you feel, your thoughts, what you do, or your relationships with others. Reflect on how these insights are helping you grow and heal.

5. How did I practice self-care?

Review the self-care practices you engaged in this week. How consistent were you with your daily healing routine? Which activities made you feel most nurtured and supported? Write down any patterns or observations about your self-care habits.

6. What are my goals for next week?

Set intentions for the upcoming week. What specific goals do you want to achieve? These can be related to your personal growth, self-care practices, or any other areas of your life. Write down your goals and the steps you'll take to accomplish them.

7. Who or what am I grateful for?

Take a moment to reflect on gratitude. Who or what are you thankful for this week? It could be people, experiences, or small joys in your life. Write down your thoughts to foster appreciation and positivity.

8. What can I do differently next week?

Consider any changes or modifications you would like to make for the upcoming week. This might involve trying new self-care practices, altering your routine, or approaching challenges differently. Note down your plans to keep them at the top of your mind.

9. How did I connect with my inner child?

Reflect on any moments when you felt connected to your inner child. Did you engage in activities that brought you joy or comfort? How did you nurture and care for your inner child? Write down these experiences and any feelings that arose.

10. What affirmations resonated with me this week?

Remember the positive affirmations you used throughout the week. Which ones struck the closest chord with you? How did they impact your mindset and emotions? Write down the affirmations that were especially meaningful and consider incorporating them into your routine for the next week.

WEEKLY REFLECTION SHEET

Use this sheet to record your reflections at the end of each week. Print it out or recreate it in your journal to track your progress and set intentions for the coming week.

Week from _____ to _____

1. What went well this week?

_____

_____

_____

_____

_____

2. What challenges did I face?

_____

_____

_____

_____

_____

3. How did I handle stress and difficult emotions?

_____

_____

_____

_____

_____

4. What did I learn about myself?

_____

_____

_____

_____

_____

5. How did I practice self-care?

_____

_____

_____

_____

_____

6. What are my goals for next week?

_____

_____

_____

_____

_____

7. Who or what am I grateful for?

_____

_____

_____

_____

_____

8. What can I do differently next week?

_____

_____

_____

_____

_____

9. How did I connect with my inner child?

_____

_____

_____

_____

_____

10. What affirmations resonated with me this week?

_____

_____

_____

_____

_____

One effective strategy to maintain a connection to your healing process is to reflect on your past week. You can gain valuable insights, celebrate your progress, and pinpoint areas for improvement by following these prompts and recording your thoughts. By dedicating some time each week to these reflection exercises, you will discover that you are becoming more resilient, self-aware, and stronger. Never forget that this is your path and that each step you take will bring you one step closer to living a happier, healthier life.

THE

INNER CHILD

HEALING

WORKBOOK

A Self-Love Journey of Inner Awareness with CBT and Shadow Work to Integrate Your Authentic Self and Overcome Emotional Traumas, Blocks, Abuse, and Abandonment

Scarlett Kent

WORKBOOK INTRODUCTION

To maximize your inner child healing journey, use a separate journal for recording thoughts, emotions, and exercise responses. A dedicated space for self-reflection allows you to track progress, revisit insights, and observe patterns over time.

Set Up Your Journal:

- Designate a section per chapter for a structured record.
- Date each entry to track chronological evolution.
- Reserve space for additional thoughts and spontaneous reflections.
- Jot down realizations, aha moments, or newfound self-awareness.
- Capture emotions during exercises for deeper understanding.
- Reflect on the exercise impact on your current emotional state.
- Note changes in perspectives, attitudes, or behaviors.
- Monitor patterns or recurring themes throughout the journey.

Incorporating this journaling practice enhances the workbook's effectiveness, creating a personalized narrative of your healing journey. Embrace the process, remembering that healing is a gradual, transformative experience.

CHAPTER ONE

EXPLORE YOUR PAST AND WHO YOU HAVE BEEN

Those of us who go through abrupt life changes are aware that they sometimes give us the impression that we stepped through a door as one person and came out entirely different. While some can fully realize the nature and severity of the transition they've undergone right away, most people require time and a prolonged period of thought.

Of course, many have no desire to delve into the past, so they try not to think about it. However, a common goal in later adulthood is identifying and interpreting life's turning moments.

Last summer, my parents moved to a new home, and I had to carry boxes full of old notebooks, stories, artwork, and terrible pictures over to my apartment. It's unbelievable how the good pictures we kept turned out to be the kind I would erase from my phone right now. The pleasure of being a Virgo! I carefully stored them in cabinets and closets, promising to take my time sorting through them and deciding what to keep and what to throw away. Naturally, this has been out of sight and mind ever since. It's one of those things that occasionally crosses my mind, only to be put aside by the thought that it will require a significant amount of mental and physical energy. Furthermore, I was undecided as to whether it was worthwhile to review these items.

Since I try to live in the present so much, it seemed odd to me to throw myself into the past and run into all those old versions of myself. Could I become more present by delving into the past? Would it bring me, in a good or bad way, back to things I had forgotten (or tried to forget)? Although the answers are still a mystery, I couldn't help but think of all these old things that had been hidden but kept close by. I took them out, analyzed them, and thought about them for the last several weeks. Some of the things I learned are the following:

As time passes, wounds tend to mend

Many of the issues I wrote about in the past turned out to be minor or, in case they weren't, have become much easier to deal with. It was comforting to revisit these past pains and see how much had faded or disappeared. No matter what challenges you face now, things will change, and you will get through them.

I am the same

Observing how much of a mirror image I was of myself from then was unexpected. It's lovely to see that I was always writing and painting in one manner or another, especially considering the evolution. I've always found quotes and lyrics fascinating, and I used to decorate my notebooks and journals with them. I was constantly seeking a deeper understanding of myself and trying to figure out why things were the way they were (it was eye-opening to learn about the less-than-stellar traits that also persist).

I am completely different

Even though I'm still the same in many ways, I've changed and matured significantly (as everyone does). We can lose sight of how far we've come as we live in the present and don't have access to the past. Reflecting on my past has made me appreciate where I am now and hopeful about the areas of my life that I wish were different. I've changed a lot, even though it's required time and work. This gives me optimism that I'll have more freedom to make changes in the future. Thinking back on your progress can be strangely motivating, particularly if you can read what you wrote about a particular period in your own words.

Observe patterns

As I read and thought, so many positive and negative patterns kept coming to me. The number of practices I still use now is astounding to me. It opened my eyes and forced me to consider carefully which patterns I want to continue to use and which ones I should change. Even if you don't journal, you can still benefit from observing recurring patterns and determining whether they are valuable to you now. Doing something isn't necessary just because you've always done it.

Memories are just stories

Every memory you have is shaped by your particular viewpoint, which considers both the past and the present. Going back over the old memories and writing down my thoughts about them as I went along made me realize how much of the stuff we save in our heads as memories are just a collection of stories, some of which are true and some of which are not. After reading them again, things make more sense. It's almost as if you can see right through your former self to understand the feelings and how they may have shaped the memories. Examining the old memories allowed me to realize that memories aren't facts, which is a crucial lesson to remember in the present moment.

You are ignorant of your ignorance

I wish I could hug my carefree younger self and reassure her. I want her to know everything will work out, even though it won't always go as planned or how she hoped. Sometimes, I also want to sit down with her and give her a hard talk, sharing everything I've learned and wish she had known at the time. However, that's the nature of life — you never know what you don't know. All you can do is make the most of the information that is at your disposal. Thinking back on this helped me realize that I still have a lot to learn and that it's acceptable for me to be satisfied with the knowledge I now possess.

Keep the handwritten stuff

This is a brief yet significant lesson. When I was going through the boxes of old notes, pictures, and goofy little cards, I discovered that the things that individuals had taken a great deal of time to write were the ones that had the most value. Any card with just a signature was thrown in the trash, but handwritten notes, love letters, and the silly little drawings that my best friend and I used to make when we were kids… All those things still hold a special meaning for me, and help me understand not only the people around me but also myself. This brings me to the following point.

Give yourself extra time to jot it down

I wish I had written down more thoughts, created more art, and recorded truly meaningful experiences. I was in such awe at the time that I couldn't fathom losing these memories or not preserving them in written form. Even though I know that not everyone enjoys writing or creating art, I believe there is value in simply jotting down a few lines throughout noteworthy life experiences. The process is quick, and it can shed light on who you are (and how you've changed) in ways that reminiscence alone can't. It's also a tool for reflection and awareness since I felt that writing down or putting my feelings on paper or a screen helped me a lot at the time (a sort of at-home therapy).

I'm curious to know if you currently keep or have kept in the past a journal or diary. Would you be open to reviewing it once more? Is it worth another glance from you? In that case, how does it make you feel? Or would you write it down, and then keep it out of your mind?

However, here's a fun practice to try if you don't journal yet: picture every year of your life as a book. What would be the title of each book? Despite how challenging this is, I think it's a great way to reflect and I'd recommend it to everyone.

Exercise: Analysis of myself

Have you experienced satisfaction in your life recently?   ○ Yes   ○ No

Do you often feel overwhelmed by daily pressures?   ○ Yes   ○ No

Do you openly express your deepest feelings?   ○ Yes   ○ No

Are you satisfied with your self-esteem?   ○ Yes   ○ No

Are you afraid of the judgment of others?   ○ Yes   ○ No

Do you find it challenging to forgive yourself for past mistakes?   ○ Yes   ○ No

Do you avoid emotional situations?   ○ Yes   ○ No

Have you noticed negative behavioral patterns in your life?   ○ Yes   ○ No

Do you constantly seek approval from others?   ○ Yes   ○ No

Do you feel adequate compared to expectations?   ○ Yes   ○ No

Do you explore your passions and interests?   ○ Yes   ○ No

Do you take care of your mental well-being?   ○ Yes   ○ No

Are you open to accepting your vulnerabilities?   ○ Yes   ○ No

Have you addressed harmful behaviors?   ○ Yes   ○ No

Does your routine contribute to your well-being?   ○ Yes   ○ No

Do you have positive relationships?   ○ Yes   ○ No

Are you motivated to pursue personal goals?   ○ Yes   ○ No

Do you know when to ask for help?   ○ Yes   ○ No

Do you easily let go of the past?   ○ Yes   ○ No

Do you have clear goals for the future?   ○ Yes   ○ No

Do you tend to rebel without reason?   ○ Yes   ○ No

Do you often hope without apparent reason?   ○ Yes   ○ No

Do you consider yourself a good person?   ○ Yes   ○ No

Do you often criticize yourself and others?   ○ Yes   ○ No

Are you defensive in interactions?   ○ Yes   ○ No

Do you distrust others without reason?   ○ Yes   ○ No

Do you often experience stress or nervousness without a clear cause?   ○ Yes   ○ No

Do you often think catastrophically?   ○ Yes   ○ No

Are your relationships often conflictual?   ○ Yes   ○ No

Do you avoid social situations?   ○ Yes   ○ No

Exercise: Mapping your timeline

Description: Create a timeline of the crucial moments in your life to start your inner child healing process. Think back on the significant events — both good and bad — that have molded the person you are now. By doing this exercise, you'll be able to recognize critical events, patterns, and triggers that could be connected to your inner child. Use images, symbols, or colors to represent the emotional tone of each event.

Instructions:

Gather materials: Get a sizable piece of paper, markers, and any other supplies you want to use.

Establish a timeline: Draw a horizontal line on the paper that represents your life from your birth to the present.

Mark essential events: To indicate both positive and bad important events, use symbols or brief descriptions throughout the timeline. Add significant moments, obstacles, and benchmarks.

Color code emotions: Use different colors to convey the various emotional tones of each event. Use warm colors, for instance, for positive experiences and cool colors for difficult ones.

Reflect: Take a moment to step back and examine your timeline, looking for any patterns, clusters, or gaps. What conclusions can you make based on this graphic depiction of your life?

Exploring connections between past and present

We are the total sum of our past. Our emotional responses to the past directly impact our lives today. We can understand what motivates our life patterns when we look within and find those feelings we still harbor.

When we cling to unpleasant emotions instead of letting them go, we end up in physical pain. We feel the physical experience of those emotions. Maybe the emotions we're holding cause our throats to feel constricted, our stomachs to feel knotted or empty, or our backs to hurt. We can identify the emotions causing those feelings by paying attention to them.

Our emotions and feelings are, in every way, our natural guidance system. Every emotion has value and is essential. They support and mentor us in identifying and addressing our needs to live happy, healthy, and purposeful lives. That improves all sensations and emotions! But our world often views a wide range of emotions and feelings negatively. To numb these so-called negative emotions, we are also often administered medicines. They can provide us with short-term relief, but they can't meet our emotional demands.

Because we lack the cognitive ability to understand our emotions and feelings when we are very young, we often struggle to meet, resolve, and satisfy our emotional demands in a healthy and beneficial way. Therefore, whether on purpose or accidentally, emotions that go unfulfilled, unresolved, or unsatisfied — emotions we ignore, numb, or divert our attention from — continue to manifest, and can materialize as physically unhealthy conditions, illnesses, or diseases.

Emotional Resonance

Emotions are all just energy in action. Humans have complex emotions and are constantly filled with emotional energy and sensations. Problems arise when emotional energy is trapped, locked, and mangled inside us rather than let go through us, smoothly and freely.

According to physics, everything in the world vibrates at a specific frequency. Similar frequencies allow two things to vibrate collectively in response to a similar resonance.

This is also true of emotional resonance. The cells of our body hold our memories, ideas, emotions, and feelings. We have quick flashbacks when a scenario, incident, or event from the past connects with a situation, incident, or event from the present. These thoughts, feelings, emotions, and stored memories are energized and carried over into the present. In a sense, we are reliving our past.

The issue arises when unpleasant emotions and sensations are associated with stored memories. A certain situation, occurrence, or event can be likened to re-energizing and re-activating an unresolved, dissatisfied, or unhealed wound if it resonates with an uncomfortable former memory, despite having a different content. Like putting salt on an injury, it stings. Furthermore, an unhealed wound tends to become more and more poisoned with time as it vibrates into our current life, triggered even by minor issues.

When we're released from the emotional moorings of the past, we can sail freely and peacefully in the present. We no longer live like volcanoes waiting to erupt at the slightest disturbance and we regain authority over our lives.

CHAPTER TWO

CONNECTING WITH YOUR INNER CHILD

Last weekend, I was driving through the country, one of my favorite places to think — or, rather, to ruminate — and I noticed that my thoughts kept returning to a conversation I had with a friend and that I later regretted. As I was driving through the beautiful scenery, I was secretly reprieving myself for speaking too loud and out of turn with my friend. The inner scolding never stopped. It appears I was scolding a younger (inner) version of myself who had done something bad.

Then, I felt a strong force strike me. I realized that I would never speak to Steve — my beloved son — in the same manner that I was speaking to myself. Instead, I'd be curious and ask him what he could do differently next time. I'd be understanding and composed while he worked through the situation.

My inner child deserves my unwavering affection, too! That's when I realized how to reconnect with my inner child, and I want to share that knowledge with you so you can do the same.

Everyone has an inner child. This is the side of ourselves that emerged when we were children and we didn't get what we needed. Most of the time, we have multiple inner children rather than just one. And these aspects of ourselves shape the way we behave in the world (mine had made me a little too aggressive toward my friend!).

It takes practice to know how to connect and communicate compassionately with our inner children. In this chapter, I outline the exact steps you may take to begin doing it more regularly.

Techniques for stronger inner child connection

While establishing a connection with your inner child, it's important to consider the best interests of your past and present self. Another thing to keep in mind is to pretend you're a child engaging with your younger self.

Those of us who experienced abuse could find that we are kinder to others than we are to ourselves. Thus, maybe you could be more compassionate and kinder if you could see the child you once were right in front of you.

Going back to a traumatic event isn't what inner child work is about. So, when you interact with your younger self, try to remember specific memories, but don't repeat them. This isn't a re-traumatization process; rather, it's a path of self-discovery and healing.

Keep in mind that this process isn't meant to be an escape or an avoidance mechanism. In other words, try not to let your inner child take over so much that you start ignoring your adult responsibilities and life. Look for a balance that feels right for you.

Furthermore, try to avoid the company of those who believe that engaging in inner child work or reaching out to your past selves is foolish, childish, or even insane. Reconnecting with your inner child, having fun, and rediscovering your childhood is actually a healthy and liberating emotional release.

1. Embrace your inner child

If we're open, we can communicate with our inner children. However, you might struggle if you are unsure or opposed to the idea.

If you're not comfortable with inner child work, try to think of this concept as an exploration of your former experiences and self. Make an effort to recognize and acknowledge your inner child. When you do, give them the respect, love, and kindness that both of you deserve. Embrace and care for your inner child in a way that your parents were unable to.

2. Let your inner child guide you

Recognizing your inner child requires you to listen to them. This helps you make both the past and the present meaningful. Consider listening to your inner child. Did they experience feelings of helplessness, guilt, shame, humiliation, anger, abandonment, rejection, insecurity, or vulnerability? What caused such feelings to arise?

Should you be able to link specific emotions to the corresponding childhood experiences, you might see that comparable situations in your adult life elicit the same feelings.

It's critical to acknowledge and embrace your inner child. Their worries may appear trivial or absurd to you but keep in mind that a lot of the problems we face now probably have their roots in unresolved childhood difficulties. Thus, hearing about your earlier problems may enable you to have a deeper understanding of the problems you are facing now.

When I was a child, for instance, my mother's anger, unhappiness, or irritation would always signal the possibility of abuse — verbal or physical. Now, as an adult, I am triggered by other people's emotions and body language that I perceive as upset, anger, or annoyance.

3. Observe your inner child

Seeing how your inner child behaves is another step in acknowledging them. Children often misbehave because they are unable to control their emotions. Were you often evasive, hostile, aggressive, silent, reserved, alone, or distracted? What emotions could have led you to behave in that manner?

My parents and several relatives used to refer to me as a "troublesome" or "bad" child when I was little. I can still clearly recall my belligerent, boisterous, and tantrum-throwing behavior when I didn't get things my way. Therefore, I spent my childhood blaming myself for my hurts, lack of friends, and lack of love from others.

But as I grew older, my perspective on things began to shift. I was never called a terrible kid by my grandmother. Conversely, she often complimented my young self, saying I was wise, helpful, and all-around wonderful. Why? My grandmother was the only person who showed me love, patience, and care. She was the only person who had faith in me.

I don't believe I was a bad child in the end. To be honest, I don't believe that any child is awful. Some kids just don't have enough love in their lives or don't have the resources or guidance to deal with it.

Therefore, consider how your abusive parents or environment may have contributed to any thoughts you may have had about yourself, such as being bad, abnormal, or that something is wrong with you.

4. Write a letter to your inner child

If you want to help your inner child see things from an adult's perspective, try writing down a letter to them, to give them a better grasp of their potential.

For example, I can reassure my inner child that she wasn't a nasty child by sending a letter to her. I can tell her how hard she tried and all the good things she did, but it was never good enough. And it's not at all her fault.

You can tell your inner child that they are not to blame for the abuse they experience. Alternatively, you can reassure them that good things will come eventually. By doing this, you can help your inner child make sense of some things and possibly ease some of your residual pain. Perhaps it will allow you to come to some sort of resolution. Perhaps it will help you release some of the shame and guilt you've been carrying around for so long.

5. Engage in a dialogue with your inner child

One way to communicate with one's inner child is to listen to them. This can aid your understanding of their viewpoint and how it may have influenced the person you are today.

You have three options: write everything down, talk aloud, or have the discussion in your head, whichever suits you best. Treat them with the same respect and kindness that you would have with any other child as you converse with them.

How you wish to communicate is up to you. You may turn this into a Q&A session and ask questions about your early years. After that, answer them as if you were your inner child. Alternatively, strike up a casual discussion and see where it goes.

By talking to your inner child, you might be able to unearth harmful habits, events, or feelings from the past that you may have repressed. A link between your younger and present selves can also be formed and strengthened through this process.

By developing the practice of talking to and listening to your inner child, you can discover more effective strategies for meeting your needs from childhood and now.

6. Look to children for guidance

Maybe you can ask other children for advice if you're having problems connecting, listening, chatting, or engaging in any other activity with your inner child. They might be children you know from friends and relatives or your own children.

Engage in conversation with them to see if they can jog your memories of earlier years. Try to listen, watch, and converse with other kids to get a sense of what your childhood self would have been like — and just do the same with your inner child. Try to view the world from their perspective. Engage in fun activities with them. Playing any kind of game with kids has its advantages.

7. Journal as your inner child

You can manage difficult or confusing feelings and events by keeping a journal. In order to embrace your inner child, try journaling. Take on the perspective that you had when you were a child. You don't need to write with excessive care or thought. Try to just let the ideas come to you as they arise. Avoid self-censorship or perfectionism, as journaling should be. Just write.

If it helps, try focusing on a particular period of time or age that you remember well. This may be a time of your childhood when you were most happy and carefree, or it could be a moment when you were really struggling.

You can write about a specific event. Alternatively, you might choose to use one of the following journaling prompts:

- What is your most treasured memory? Why? Who showed up? Where were you? What feelings did you experience?
- How did you relax or comfort yourself when you felt sad or scared as a little one?
- What do you enjoy doing in your free time? How frequently are you doing it? What is it about it that you find enjoyable?
- How are you treated by your parents? What is your opinion of their behavior toward you?
- What are some typical emotions you experience? What appears to set them off?
- Where is your ideal vacation spot? Why?
- In the future, what do you see yourself doing? Why?
- What are your dreams?
- With whom do you feel happy and safe? Why do you feel that way when you're around them?
- Recall a time when you were terribly scared, hurt, or furious. How did that happen?
- How would you describe your self-esteem? If you had to define yourself in just three words, what would they be and why?

Think about the answers you may give if you were to ask these questions to both your current adult self and your younger self. Next, consider how and why your responses, viewpoints, or feelings might differ.

Do your dreams remain the same? Are you now the person you aspired to be as an adult? When you think back on your childhood, how do you feel about how your parents treated you?

8. Find keepsakes from your childhood

Observing objects that hold sentimental value, films, yearbooks, toys, drawings, and other keepsakes from your childhood can evoke feelings of nostalgia and make the reconnection with your inner child easier.

To further develop your bond, you can even look at items from that time that aren't necessarily yours or connected to you. You may play a game, watch a show, or research things or trends that were popular at the time.

While you work on this, think about your feelings and the state of life at the time. Next, consider how that particular point in time influenced your current circumstances.

9. Rediscover the joys of childhood

When you were a kid, I bet you did a lot of cool stuff. You did those things only because you wanted to; you weren't forced to. In order to reconnect with your inner child, consider doing them as an adult right now.

Indulge in some of your old favorite foods, games, movies, or books. Craft something, do science experiments, engage in sand play, or blow bubbles.

In my opinion, this isn't childish at all. This is about rediscovering the joys of childhood and experiencing the world through fresh eyes.

Consider what you've always wanted to do and find an opportunity to do it now if you weren't able to enjoy many fun activities as a child because you didn't feel like it or weren't allowed to.

Perhaps you've always wanted to go to a certain location, take up a particular hobby, buy a certain item, or engage in a specific game. Maybe you were never given the opportunity to do these things as a child. It may seem like you've grown up physically, but you can try to make up for the things you were denied as a child.

Make an effort to fulfill a few of your childhood dreams — you don't have to go to extremes.

10. Enjoy yourself!

The countless duties that come with becoming an adult cause major anxiety and stress. However, having fun and unwinding are crucial for your mental health.

Reconnecting with your inner child and scheduling fun activities can help in your healing process, regardless of how happy or unhappy your early years were. Perhaps it can ease the hurt of having missed out on the childhood joy that you deserved.

It's not necessary to engage in classic childhood hobbies like going down a slide or blowing bubbles, though you can if you find them enjoyable. However, as an adult, you are free to pursue interests outside of work.

Not everything needs to be productive or profitable. The time you enjoy wasting is not wasted, as goes one of my favorite sayings. Additionally, engaging in enjoyable activities and having fun improves your mood and, consequently, your health. Therefore, it isn't useless or pointless at all.

Try to enjoy the small things in life as well. Recognize how ice cream or a small present may brighten a child's day. Incorporate that into your daily routine.

Exercise: Visualization Journey

Description: Embark on a transformative inner journey by engaging in a Visualization Journey. This exercise fosters a deeper connection with your inner child, offering insights and messages that contribute to a more compassionate self-understanding.

Instructions:

- Prepare your Space: Find a quiet, comfortable space where you can lie or sit down without interruptions.
- Deep Breathing: Start with a few deep breaths to relax your mind and body.
- Close your Eyes: Imagine a door that leads to your inner child's world. Open the door and step into a vibrant, safe space from your childhood.
- Explore and Connect: Take a mental journey through this space, exploring significant places or moments from your past. Try to engage all your senses, noticing colors, smells, and textures.
- Meet your Inner Child: As you explore, visualize your younger self. Approach them with curiosity and openness. Ask your inner child what they need or want to express. Listen and respond with love and understanding.

Exploring emotions tied to childhood experiences

In this section, we'll talk about the emotions associated with your early years. This is crucial because it clarifies the essence of your identity and the ways in which your past shapes who you are now. You can learn more about yourself by exploring your past because your feelings are like the colors that paint your life.

Recall your early years. What emotions surface when you think back at those formative years? Perhaps you remember the excitement of something new, the warmth of family, or the delight of a birthday. You may also recall moments of frustration, loneliness, or anger. For this section, we want you to identify and label every emotion you had at that time. This helps to untangle the complex web of your past.

Emotions aren't merely transient phenomena. They are like many threads that are woven together with our experiences. You're making significant progress toward understanding your past by identifying and labeling these emotions. Think about journaling your feelings as you go through this adventure. This not only proves your discoveries but also offers guidance when navigating your emotions.

Childhood is full of feelings. It's a period when the world is a place of limitless discovery; joy may feel incredibly large, and sadness can feel overwhelming. Accept and value every emotion you experienced, including the times you laughed, cried, felt scared, or excited. Our goal is to embrace all of these feelings without assigning them a positive or negative value. Every emotion contributes to the unique picture of who you are.

Impact on Present Emotions

As we explore your past, it's important to recognize how your early experiences continue to influence your present emotions. Imagine your current feelings as ripples on the surface of a pond, with the rocks causing those ripples hidden beneath. Which events from your early years caused those ripples in your life?

When anything reminds you of the past, especially in the present, you may experience again some of the same emotions. Understanding these connections empowers you to act thoughtfully rather than just instinctively. Understanding the source of your emotions gives you greater awareness and resilience as you move through today's life.

Imagine that your life is a song with recurring patterns that resemble well-known tunes. In this section, we want you to explore these patterns and the triggers associated with particular emotions. Are there some things or circumstances that always give you a particular feeling? Finding these patterns enables you to understand the emotional rhythm of your feelings.

Recognizing patterns is similar to knowing your life's melody. Observing these patterns will help you compose a more harmonic song. Consider any recurring themes or emotions that spring to mind when you reflect on your past experiences. This awareness functions as a kind of road map for your journey of self-discovery.

Expression and repression

Emotional expression standards are commonly grounded in childhood. Some families can teach their children to keep their emotions inside, while others might encourage open communication of emotions. Remember how your family and society handled emotions as you reflect on things from the past.

Were you allowed to express your happiness, or did your tears make others uncomfortable? You can understand better why you manage your emotions the way you do by taking a look at how they were expressed or not expressed. Remember that experiencing emotional expression is an inherent aspect of being

human, and this exploration encourages you to embrace that fact. As we grow, we all learn coping mechanisms for the highs and lows of life. While some methods may not be beneficial, others may be. Consider for a moment how you handled situations when you were younger.

Did you spend time with loved ones, indulge in your creative side, or even isolate yourself from others? Understanding these coping mechanisms enables you to recognize the strength that saw you through difficult circumstances. It also allows you to evaluate if these methods of handling problems continue to be effective for you or whether there is an opportunity for alternative strategies.

Self-compassion and validation

In your emotional journey, every feeling matters. Accept the fact that your emotions are real, no matter what anyone may say. Practice self-compassion as you go through your childhood feelings and emotions.

Imagine yourself as a compassionate observer of your younger self's feelings. Recognize that your emotions, both then and today, are a natural part of being human, and offer words of consolation and understanding. Validation and self-compassion create a safe environment that allows you to heal, let go of judgment, and accept the authenticity of your emotional path.

It takes courage to face your childhood emotions, and this bravery offers the possibility of healing. As you reflect on your emotional journey, take into account some possible healing options. This might include talking to someone, engaging in mindfulness exercises, or coming up with creative ways to communicate your feelings.

Like speaking with a counselor, therapy provides an organized setting for understanding and processing feelings. Meditation and other forms of mindfulness practice keep you alert and focused. Whether it's through writing, painting, or dancing, being creative allows you to release and express pent-up emotions.

As we get to the end of our exploration of childhood emotions, remember that this journey is a part of your inner child's work. The emotions you discover are like your inner child's cries for understanding. Deep healing and self-discovery are within reach when you combine this emotional exploration with the more general concept of inner child work.

The memories of your past emotions are trapped inside your inner child. You create the conditions for effective healing by handling these emotions with compassion and understanding. Remember that learning about yourself is a continuous process, and each step you take enriches the vibrant mosaic that is your inner world.

Exercise: Emotional Journaling

Description: Dive in the process of self-discovery with Emotion Journaling. This exercise encourages self-reflection and validation, fostering a compassionate understanding of your younger self and the lasting impact of these emotions on your present experiences.

Instructions:

- Recall Childhood Experiences: Think about specific childhood memories or experiences that evoke strong emotions. It could be joy, sadness, anger, or fear.

_____

_____

_____

- Express Emotions: Write down the emotions associated with each memory. Be detailed and specific about how you felt during those moments.

_____

_____

_____

- Seek Recurring Themes: Analyze the feelings you've recorded for any distinct patterns. Are there particular situations or relationships that repeatedly evoke certain emotions?

_____

_____

_____

- Reflect and Validate: Reflect on your journal entries and validate your younger self's emotions. Offer self-compassion and understanding, acknowledging the impact of these experiences on your present emotions.

_____

_____

_____

CHAPTER THREE

IDENTIFYING TRAUMA, NEGATIVE EXPERIENCES, AND HEALING EMOTIONAL WOUNDS

Almost everyone experiences trauma throughout their lives. However, what are the enduring effects of trauma and negative experiences? Do these events have an impact on us for the rest of our lives?

Yes, there are a lot of negative long-term impacts of trauma that follow a person for the rest of their life. The repercussions are more severe for some people than for others. The best course of action is to try to process your trauma with professional help and guidance. Recognizing and understanding your trauma can also help you in making a change.

Understanding and identifying trauma and emotional wounds

Not everything in the past stays where it should. If you were traumatized as a child, it might surprise you to learn that the traumatic issues you faced are still present in the adult age. You could be worried that the trauma you experienced as a child will negatively impact your happiness, relationships, or even your career. Perhaps you're unsure where to start on your journey to recovery. Recently, you haven't felt like yourself. And you've been thinking if this is the fault of the trauma from your childhood that you never got over. You thought it was over. But could your adult life be affected by your trauma? Do you feel as if everything is upside down? If that's the case, why now?

Why now? The question seems to be somewhat substantial. You've done everything in your power in order to overcome that issue. Most of the time you even managed to successfully block it out. However, you've been experiencing anxiety again recently, occasionally on the verge of panic. Feelings of sadness and depression are beginning to take control. Maybe you're even considering isolating yourself.

In what way could your trauma remain unresolved? What's happening here?

Unresolved trauma: what is it?

What is unresolved trauma? You told yourself it happened long ago and now you're moving on. Could that possibly be not enough?

Perhaps you also went to therapy. How on earth could you still be in pain? The trauma you experienced as a child is rooted deep within you. It kind of becomes a part of you, like a tattoo.

Even if the memories are suppressed and unconscious, they still are nevertheless deeply grounded in your symptoms, interpersonal difficulties, and low self-esteem. Due to their long-standing sense of isolation, many children who have experienced trauma often seek solace in trying to solve problems independently.

The problem is that when you're alone, you can do only so much. The most severe repercussions of childhood trauma often remain unresolved. You may wonder, "What if I've already tried therapy?" Yeah, it's a bummer. Since a lot of therapists aren't specialists in treating childhood trauma, you need to be addressed at the root of your early traumas.

A template for resolving deep childhood trauma doesn't exist. You're an individual with unique experiences that have shaped who you are.

Unfortunately, the causes of your childhood trauma remain unsolved. Those symptoms may temporarily disappear. However, the stress that upsets your emotions or something that reminds you too much of your past trauma can force you to relive the original events.

Why "the past" isn't always the past.

Even if your childhood trauma is officially in the past, it won't be possible to move on from it until you have a thorough understanding of how it continues to influence your present relationships, experiences, and symptoms.

We are compelled to repeat ourselves, even when we make an effort not to. For this reason, you may find yourself in relationships that bring back memories of past traumas.

Your symptoms or habits may show up in different ways, and once again, these are unique to you. Never let the past be just the past; what really counts is moving forward.

Your childhood trauma may remain unresolved until you seek assistance in identifying the specific ways in which your past experiences continue to impact your present.

What leads to childhood trauma?

In some cases, trauma is obvious, such as with physical or sexual abuse. Be that as it may, many types of childhood trauma may go unrecognized.

Terrible experiences can manifest in a variety of ways, including neglect, severe childhood illness, a learning disability that leads to self-doubt, too many siblings, a parent who is emotionally distant, anxious, or inaccessible, or even your parents' own terrible experiences from their childhood.

Perhaps you had more than one of these experiences: your parents suffered from childhood trauma; they were emotionally distant or unavailable; they lost a parent; you had a learning disability; you had too many siblings... possibly a combination of all these factors.

Neglect throughout childhood refers to not having your physical or emotional needs met. This might have happened as a result of your parents' stress and distraction. Alternatively, it could be due to their own mental illnesses, possibly forcing adult responsibilities on you, like looking after the other children or performing a lot more housework than a child should.

Whatever the reason, your desires for support and affection were ignored, rejected, or met with intense animosity. Never should a parent's needs force a child to be exploited. Prioritizing a child's emotional and physical needs is important. If your parents failed to do so, you were neglected.

Being abandoned or losing a parent at a young age is traumatizing. This kind of loss is profound, regardless of how well-cared you were by other family members or your surviving parents. Your sense of loss endures far more deeply within you if your sadness isn't seen, heard, or allowed. You could still require some time to process your loss because you discovered far too early that a loved one who is needed can suddenly disappear or be taken away from you. The fear of losing is rooted within you from a young age. Losing a parent at any age is difficult, but especially when you're in your twenties. Since need and closeness imply the potential of loss, you can be afraid of closeness.

Most cases of unresolved childhood trauma have a negative impact on anxiety levels and self-esteem.

Has a serious sickness plagued you since you were a child? If that was the case, you were likely hospitalized or kept isolated at home. Being cut off from regular social activities meant that you were likely lonely and perhaps even scared of being different.

Maybe, as a result, you now lack social confidence and are unsure of your place in the group. Hospitalization also entails parental separation, traumatic medical procedures, and a lot of worries. You might experience chronic anxiety as a result of this. It helps if your parents are there for you and offer support and if your bonds with them are safe. If not, you might now feel insecurity in important relationships.

If you had learning difficulties, dyslexia, ADHD, or any other type of learning disability, you probably felt different from the other kids or negatively compared to them.

Living with learning difficulties might be especially challenging if you don't receive enough support and your problems go untreated. Many smart kids eventually come to believe they aren't.

This severely damages your perception of yourself. It's possible that you made a lot of effort to get better and better while battling uncontrollable obstacles. Or maybe you surrendered and gave in. Either you continue to strive for perfection, always looking forward to satisfying people, or you just never feel good enough. You can also feel like you're always falling behind and are unable to catch up. Even if you believe your learning difficulties are resolved, their effects may still affect you.

Were you born in a large family? Did you ever feel insufficient for everyone else? That is often the case if you had many siblings. There really aren't enough resources, especially when you were all born so close to each other. And particularly if your mom was exhausted, stressed out, and preoccupied with your siblings who always seemed to have more needs than you. Or, if you were the eldest, you were supposed to watch out for the little ones. Growing up with multiple siblings as a child can be traumatizing, regardless of how caring you think your family was. Perhaps you felt lost among the many. Not heard or seen. Isolated, pushed aside, and left out. A child in this situation may experience emotional neglect and feel unloved.

You might even believe that in order to receive love, you had to put your wants aside or show others generosity. You can also have a constant yearning for the love you believe you can't and will never find.

The consequences of having too many siblings are magnified when the mother is unresponsive or distant. A parent who is unreachable causes trauma. Children must be appreciated, seen, heard, held, and given emotional support. The consequences of watching, waiting, and wanting your emotions to be acknowledged might be lifelong.

Perhaps you're unsure about being loved and cautious about your demands. Or maybe you learned to maintain your distance and lower your expectations. Perhaps you had an overanxious parent. One who hid from others, was terrified, thought the worst, or lacked trust. A child may internalize their parents' anxiety, leading to constant anxiety and similar fears, often without even being aware of it.

Experiencing trauma was likely common for parents who were anxious or emotionally distant as well. Certain traumas can even span across generations. If your parents experienced similar trauma and that trauma was also not resolved, it gets inherited by the child, from the unconscious mind to the unconscious mind.

Children are vulnerable. You absorbed that trauma, and it also had an impact on you. Traumatized parents carry their trauma within them and therefore, they often aren't able to give you their whole attention.

Alternatively, in situations where your parents experienced a horrifying incident or scarring experience, like the Holocaust, the fear and unfathomable losses they endured may continue to haunt them and you.

All of these different trauma origins, along with their varied manifestations, can have an ongoing impact on you far into adulthood if left untreated.

How does trauma affect you in your adult life?

No matter how much you strive to leave the past behind, a traumatized child will always be a part of you, and this means that traumatic experiences as a child can sometimes permeate into your adult life. If you haven't received any adequate help or appropriate therapy to address your trauma, the child within you continues to bear the scars and anguish from your past.

Stress triggers the symptoms of your childhood trauma, even if you're not always aware of them. The same happens when something occurs in your life that reminds you, subtly or not, of something that happened to you when you were a kid. The early trauma you experienced is the direct cause of your current issues: panic attacks, depression, an eating disorder, catastrophic anxiety, relationship fears, and obsessional worries.

You may struggle with trust, have low self-esteem, worry about being judged, want to please people all the time, get frustrated easily, or persistently experience symptoms of social anxiety.

Exercise: "Reflection on Personal History"

Description: Delve into your personal history to identify and understand instances of trauma and emotional wounds. Take a quiet moment to reflect on significant life events, both positive and negative, that may have left a lasting impression. Consider relationships, major life changes, or any experience that felt overwhelming or distressing. Write down these events in your journal, describing the emotions associated with each of them. If you want to discover how your past has affected your mental health, this exercise is a good place to start.

Instructions:

- Create a Safe Space: Look for a peaceful spot where you won't be interrupted while you meditate.
- Reflect on Life Events: Consider key events from your past – relationships, family dynamics, major life changes, or any situations that felt challenging.
- Emotional Exploration: Write down the emotions connected to each event. Be honest and specific about how these experiences made you feel.
- Recognize Patterns: Examine your thoughts for common points or themes that keep popping up. Identify events that may have contributed to emotional wounds or trauma.

- Note Insights: Jot down any insights or realizations that emerge during this reflection. This exercise lays the groundwork for understanding the emotional landscape of your past.

_____

_____

_____

Things you don't realize you're doing because you're emotionally wounded

Have you ever heard that it takes longer to heal a broken heart than a broken bone? Yes, that's right! Past traumas can subtly influence our thoughts, emotions, and behaviors. Therefore, if something from a long time ago still feels fresh, it may be the driving force behind part of your current actions.

Here, we'll highlight ten indicators of emotional traumas. Our objective? To help you identify them, understand them, and begin the healing process. Now, let's get started!

1. Over-apologizing for everything

Have you ever apologized for stepping on someone else's toes or for bumping into a chair? These may be kind gestures, but over-apologizing might indicate emotional baggage.

Sometimes, after being hurt in the past, we feel as though we should stay away from any possibility of stirring up problems or upsetting people. This may cause us to apologize excessively — even for things that weren't our fault.

While owning up to mistakes is a positive thing, apologizing all the time may indicate that you aren't giving yourself the credit and room you need. Never forget that it's acceptable to maintain your position and admit when something isn't right.

2. Avoiding deep connections

There was a period when I would distance myself from everyone. Did I engage in small talk? Yes, of course. But sharing personal stories or feelings? No, never. It was then that I realized how people were being turned away by my emotional scars.

It seems that when we experience pain in the past, our hearts create an imperceptible barrier to shield themselves. We may believe: "I can't be harmed by someone if I don't get too close to them." However, we also lose out on the coziness and delight of real interactions when we do this.

It could be time to reflect on why you're doing this and determine whether any unresolved scars are preventing you from fully committing to friendships and relationships. Opening up can be frightening, but it can also be both liberating and healing.

3. Having self-doubt all the time

At one point in my life, every choice I made, no matter how minor, felt like I was climbing a mountain. Is this something I should wear? Is my work up to par? Was that a good joke?

These worries were the result of deeper emotional scars rather than actual concerns about jokes or clothes. When we experienced rejection, hurt, or criticism in the past, it's natural to begin to question our value.

This self-doubt can become like a background noise, complicating decisions at every turn. However, this doesn't imply your feelings and instincts aren't real now just because you were hurt in the past.

It's critical to recognize these self-doubting emotions and to constantly remind ourselves of our value and resilience.

4. Ignoring the pain rather than taking it out

Distractions abound in our culture today, including never-ending TV shows, mindless habits and behaviors that steal our time on social media. However, there are instances when we use these diversionary tactics to block out the pain rather than just pass the time.

It's painful but true: a lot of us use hobbies, medicines, or even our jobs as a way to numb our emotional scars rather than deal with the pain directly. It's like covering a serious gash with a band-aid: the damage is not healed.

Actually, it's terrible to face our pain. However, numbing it repeatedly just makes it worse. The process of healing starts when we discover the strength to face our pain, stay with it, come to terms with it, and ultimately figure out how to let it go.

5. Looking for validation rather than self-acceptance

Likes on a post, comments online, and nods of agreement at meetings can all become addictive, particularly when we're feeling down. We look outside of ourselves for solace and certainty, thinking that it would satisfy the emptiness.

However, the truth is that an emotionally wounded heart can't be healed by any amount of external approval. It may give you a short-lived sense of value, but it's like trying to drink salt water to relieve your thirst — it just makes you want more.

Accepting and embracing ourselves for who we are — flaws and all — instead of waiting for other people to do it for us is the true path to recovery.

6. Excessive positivity and refraining from negativity

Being the type that always sees the glass half full all the time may seem strange, but occasionally it might indicate deep emotional traumas. Avoiding negative emotions or thoughts obsessively might be a defensive mechanism, even if optimism is generally a positive quality.

It would be like painting over a stained wall without first cleaning it: the problem is still there. We deprive ourselves of the opportunity to process and recover from bad emotions by denying ourselves the opportunity to feel them.

Being consistently happy isn't the goal of true emotional balance; rather, it's about acknowledging all emotions, both positive and negative, and allowing ourselves the time and space to process and grow from them.

7. Overcompensating by being a people pleaser

Have you ever found yourself always saying yes to requests or changing your behavior and beliefs to conform to what other people think you should be doing?

This inclination toward overaccommodation in an attempt to overcompensate often is the result of emotional scars. There's a secret fear that we will be alone or rejected if we don't live up to everyone's expectations.

However, continuously going above and beyond for other people can be exhausting and cause us to lose sight of our own boundaries and desires. While seeking harmony and showing compassion for others is admirable, it's also critical to acknowledge and respect our own needs and emotions.

Always remember to put your own needs first and to say no when necessary.

8. Establishing emotional distance, even when physically close

I was physically close to loved ones, in rooms full of laughter and conversation, but I still felt very far away. Being present physically but emotionally distant is an odd feeling.

Later on, I realized that it was a defense mechanism I had unintentionally developed as a result of emotional trauma from the past. It was easier to lose myself in my own world than to run the risk of being vulnerable or harmed.

However, I was also losing out on sincere, intimate, and connecting moments because of this emotional distance. Realizing this pattern was the first step in lowering my guard and being fully present with the people I care about.

9. Seeking control in unpredictable circumstances

Although life is unpredictable, this unpredictability might feel unbearably dangerous to someone who is still healing from emotional scars. This leads to a need to have control over everything in life, including relationships, careers, and daily schedules.

Often, this need for control is an attempt to keep oneself from feeling exposed or to stop traumatic events from happening again. But holding on too tightly can stifle spontaneity and flexibility, straining relationships and limiting life experiences. Healing and leading a more fulfilling existence can be facilitated by accepting that we are not in control of everything and finding serenity in life's uncertainty.

10. Rejecting love despite your desire for it

Many of us secretly long for acceptance, affection, and connection. Ironically, though, we push it away while it's close at hand. We flinch out of fear of being hurt again, not because we don't want it. The harsh truth is that emotional scars can cause us to mistrust real intimacy and affection. What happens if they leave? What if we're not enough? These anxieties cause us to ruin relationships before they start or point out flaws in people who simply want to be with us. Refusing love doesn't protect us from pain; on the contrary, it makes us feel more alone.

A real connection can be established by embracing vulnerability and realizing that love carries risks. These ideas can help tear down these barriers.

Exercise: Deep questions to analyze wounds or negative traumas

Answer these questions aimed at bringing up events, memories, and negative feelings tied to childhood, helping you better understand your inner child and establish a connection with that inner aspect of yourself. Remember to approach these questions with kindness and compassion, allowing emotions and thoughts to surface without judgment. This exercise is an important step towards emotional awareness and healing from past wounds. If you find that the questions evoke intense feelings or emotional difficulties, consider sharing your thoughts with someone close to you to seek external support:

- Have you ever experienced a traumatic event that continues to impact your emotional life?

_____

_____

- Are there past experiences that trigger strong emotional reactions when you recall them?

_____

_____

- Have you ever felt a sense of abandonment or significant rejection in your life?

_____

_____

- Do you remember moments when you felt insecure, helpless, or unloved?

_____

_____

- Have you been bullied or mistreated during childhood or adolescence?

_____

_____

- Are there past relationships that have left unresolved emotional wounds?

_____

_____

- Have you gone through periods of significant stress or crises that have left an emotional mark?

_____

_____

- Do you engage in self-destructive habits or harmful behaviors connected to past traumas?

_____

_____

- Have you experienced significant losses that continue to cause emotional pain?

_____

_____

- Have you endured physical, sexual, or emotional violence that requires healing?

_____

_____

Introduction to healing strategies

Everyone has gone through a severe emotional wound that they felt they would never fully heal from, possibly causing them to become disconnected from all that was comfortable and familiar to them.

Let's face it: heartbreak, in whatever form it manifests, is unpleasant. This is true whether you have personally experienced heartbreak or other severe emotional pain, like the ending of a career you believed would continue forever or losing a loved one.

Emotional wounds can leave us reeling, desperate for anything that could help ease the searing agony and anguish that seems to consume every waking moment. For example, we may seek remedy, closure, answers, or an apology from someone we feel has harmed us.

But when we get through the initial gloom and confusion of whatever incident has caused such a severe psychological wound, we often get bogged down in uncertainty and self-doubt. We can experience shock and hopelessness when the resolution we so strongly want never seems to materialize.

Emotional scars can be healed

The good news is that most emotional scars eventually fade, and the majority of people heal. But healing doesn't happen instantly. It's crucial to handle the healing process with self-compassion, patience, and being careful not to put too much pressure on yourself.

Grief rewires the brain

A lot of evidence points to the idea that grief changes the brain chemistry. Heartbreak, separation, losing one's career, and losing support networks are a few circumstances that can cause grief but sadly, they aren't as commonly acknowledged as other types of grief.

That being said, many of us may feel as though we'll never be able to fully reclaim our former identities when we are experiencing intense emotional pain.

Research indicates that trauma changes people's thoughts and behaviors, for instance, but these changes don't always have to be negative; they can be difficult or cause our lives to change from what they were before, in which case we may need some help adjusting to these new realities, often through therapy.

Changes can be beneficial in that emotional scars can cause us to become more resilient, self-compassionate, patient, and understanding.

How does one get over emotional wounds?

In addition to psychological therapies, research indicates that some self-management techniques can help individuals heal from emotional scars that might be impeding their potential and holding them back.

Among these strategies are the following:

1. Recognizing and acknowledging that setbacks are normal and a necessary component of the healing process

A failure serves as a prelude to a triumph. A setback is a natural part of the healing process and an opportunity to learn what works and what doesn't.

Furthermore, a setback during the healing process from emotional traumas can teach us valuable lessons about how to improve going forward. In doing so, they provide us with the tools and the compassion to overcome any deep-rooted hurt and accept our true selves again.

Mental health experts advise people to be curious about whatever mistakes they make during their recovery and what they may learn from them rather than trying to avoid setbacks. This will help them move forward toward deeper healing and self-love.

2. Asking for help and receive support from others

Even for those who find it relatively easy to speak up about their feelings, reaching out for support and help can be difficult because it requires us to be vulnerable with our loved ones as well as strangers.

However, in order to heal, we require the help and empathy of others; we cannot do it by ourselves. Asking for help can be difficult, especially if you've had individuals violate your trust in the past. Nonetheless, leaning on a network of support can help you make sense of your experiences and offer the comfort, direction, and encouragement needed to help you heal old wounds and reduce their influence. Many psychologists think that seeking help can help people overcome feelings of guilt and inadequacy and this is just another type of self-care.

3. Making some progress in the direction of recovery

Emotional wounds may require time to heal. Nevertheless, it should come as no surprise that the majority of us are inclined to hasten the healing process in the hope that it will somehow ease some of the more intolerable symptoms. This reasoning is often motivated by the idea that the sooner these feelings are gone, the better. All of this is to be expected, and as most people will agree that it's not fun to constantly feel rejected, depressed, angry, or numb. On the other hand, the only way out is through, especially when it comes to overcoming difficult emotions and staying emotionally stable. We must first fully experience emotional wounds in order to be able to release them and heal from them.

No matter how slow we are, we can still handle the flood of emotions that inevitably arise by breaking it down into smaller, more manageable chunks. It can be scary to consider life after a catastrophic event or a severe heartbreak, but if you approach everything in little, manageable pieces — including your thoughts and emotions — you'll have more time to adjust to your new normality.

The same is true for each change you make to your way of living. Making numerous small adjustments over an extended period of time may be more beneficial than making a single, major adjustment that could make you feel even more overwhelmed.

Little, manageable adjustments to our way of thinking and our behavior might help us acquire an openness for the changes we desire without plunging in fully.

4. Being patient and compassionate with yourself

Recovery requires a lot of patience and self-compassion: these traits can encourage you to keep going when things get hard and allow you to see how far you've come. According to research, cultivating self-compassion can also lessen the symptoms of anxiety and depression while boosting resilience, optimism, and self-worth.

Emotional wounds require time to heal, as mentioned earlier. It's okay to take one step forward and two steps back some days, as long as you are kind to yourself and continue to go forward consistently.

5. Following a self-care regimen

The term self-care has gained huge popularity recently. With good reason, the term seems to pop up in every article and social media feed these days!

It can take a long time and a lot of energy to heal emotional scars; your energies might be limited as you go through the transformation process. As a result, you need to be more aware of any mental or physical symptoms you may be experiencing, such as anxiety, fatigue, aching muscles, and so on. All of them indicate that you could be pushing yourself too hard and should take it slowly.

It could be beneficial for you to keep in mind that you should treat your emotional wound as you would a physical one: make sure you eat healthily, get plenty of rest, drink plenty of water, and, if necessary, set appropriate boundaries with those you love.

6. Keeping in mind that recovery is achievable

Recovering emotionally can be a disorganized and erratic process. Even when you feel like things are getting better, a new wave of negative emotions like grief, rage, guilt, or shame can pop up at the most inconvenient times.

You could be wondering if these emotions will ever pass and if you'll be able to live a happy and peaceful life once more. It's critical to keep telling yourself that recovery is possible and that you can get through this trying time if you have overcome other obstacles in your life. Keeping track of your progress and the lessons you have learned during your healing may be beneficial, and you may choose to use them as a stepping stone for additional personal growth.

Thankfully, emotional scars can be healed in a variety of ways, and healing is achievable with the right help and care. However, you should get professional assistance if your pain has persisted for a long time, if you feel emotionally trapped, or if your feelings of rejection, sadness, or guilt aren't getting better.

Exercise: "Personalized Healing Toolbox"

Description: Empower yourself with a personalized toolbox of healing strategies to navigate the journey toward emotional well-being. This exercise encourages you to explore and choose healing techniques that resonate with you. By creating a toolbox tailored to your preferences, you improve your ability to cope with challenges and promote emotional healing.

Instructions:

- Explore Healing Techniques: Research and explore various healing strategies, such as mindfulness, therapy, journaling, art, strolling through nature, or breathing exercises.
- Identify Favorites: Select a few techniques that resonate with you. These could be activities that bring you joy, calm, or a sense of connection.
- Create Your Toolbox: In your journal or on a poster, create a visual representation of your personalized healing toolbox. Use symbols, colors, or images to represent each technique.
- Write a Healing Plan: For each chosen technique, write a brief plan on how and when you can incorporate it into your routine. Consider different strategies for various situations.

- Regularly Update: Your healing toolbox is dynamic. Regularly revisit and update it as you discover new techniques or as your preferences evolve.
- Commit to Self-Care: Incorporate these strategies into your life as part of your commitment to self-care and healing. This exercise empowers you to actively engage in your emotional well-being journey.

CHAPTER FOUR

SHADOW WORK AND INNER CHILD HEALING

I wish I had been aware of the existence of shadow work in my teen years or in my twenties. Maybe I could have saved myself from some severe emotional pain if I had begun the inner healing process at that time. However, I'm aware that everything happens for a reason, and I didn't find shadow work intriguing until I was in my late 30s.

You know, shadow work is this incredible: a life-altering practice that can aid in the discovery and healing of our deepest emotional wounds. It pushes us to face our bad feelings, be honest with ourselves, and accept every aspect of who we are, even the aspects we would prefer to ignore or deny.

We can learn to harness our dark sides and undergo inner transformation by becoming aware of the actions, ideas, and emotions that we consider inappropriate.

This chapter covers the benefits of shadow work, how to identify your own shadows, and the effective tools for using it to repair your inner child. By understanding and incorporating these aspects of our being, we can start a path toward emotional balance and enhanced self-awareness.

Advantages of understanding and working with the shadow

There are several advantages to being aware of and able to work with the shadow. It sheds light on our motivations and character traits, allowing us to make sense of the world. Examining the dark side of our psyche helps us identify patterns that were previously unknown to us and give us new insights into how we see and engage with the world. Understanding this offers an important perspective on how to make better judgments going forward.

In addition, shadow work enables us to accept our entire selves, flaws and all, so that we can go on without feeling guilty or ashamed of the things we should or shouldn't do. I don't know about you, but for years, I struggled with depression due to buried shame.

Finding and releasing these repressed feelings is a crucial first step on the path to emotional resilience and self-love. Ultimately, by understanding our shadows, we can make significant changes in our lives and access a plethora of creative potential that was previously unattainable. In my opinion, shadow work is a really useful technique for personal development.

Analyzing your triggers and recognizing unresolved wounds

Let's talk a little bit about emotional triggers, since a vital first step in the healing process is to identify your triggers and your unhealed wounds. When we recognize the things that hurt us, we can start to understand why they have such a profound effect on us and learn more effective coping mechanisms for when they happen. By allowing ourselves to be present with these unpleasant feelings without passing judgment or assigning blame, we can understand better why we act the way we do.

Examining the unhealed scars that can be the source of our triggers is also crucial. These could be traumatic experiences from childhood or other challenging events that we are still processing. By being conscious of these and taking stock of them, we can begin to make decisions with greater consideration and become more conscious of any trends that require changing. One effective method to start the healing process from within is to identify our triggers and understand where they come from.

Emotional vulnerability:

During my most recent relationship, I gained insight into how my mental health and behavior were impacted by my sensitivity. I was able to better examine and understand my triggers as a result of this life-changing encounter.

I immediately saw an emotional reaction when I was asked to be open with my partner — whether it meant exposing my deepest emotions, anxieties, or insecurities. It felt like a part of me wanted to pull away, back down, or even stop. It made me feel exposed and uneasy, which instinctively made me want to shield myself.

After gaining this awareness, I looked more closely at the underlying reasons for my reactions. I started a more in-depth process of self-analysis and contemplation in an effort to understand the causes of these triggers and how they affected my relationships. I was able to progressively peel back the layers of my emotional reactions with the support of open dialogue with close friends, self-help materials, and therapy.

I found that my tendency to back down or become silent when I felt vulnerable was a result of being rejected and damaged in the past. I had developed a defensive mechanism around unresolved childhood trauma and relationship scars, which made me feel as though my emotional health was in danger.

Acknowledging this pattern was a necessary first step toward personal development. It made it possible for me to grow in self-awareness and self-compassion. I came to see that I might build stronger and more genuine relationships with people if I faced and acknowledged my triggers.

In time, I developed the ability to share my worries and doubts honestly and openly with others, even when it's uncomfortable. I've come to see how important vulnerability is for strengthening bonds, developing emotional intimacy, and establishing trust in relationships.

I'm acquiring the bravery to confront and get past the obstacles preventing my emotional development by going after my triggers head-on.

This has also made me more determined to help people on their own paths to healing and self-discovery. I want to use my story to encourage and motivate people to face their own triggers, accept vulnerability, and build stronger, more satisfying relationships.

Exercise: "Shadow Self Exploration"

Description: Embark on a journey to explore your shadow self, the often-hidden aspects of your personality and emotions. Shadow work is an integral part of inner child healing, as it allows you to acknowledge and integrate suppressed or overlooked parts of yourself. This exercise encourages self-reflection and acceptance, paving the way for a more holistic healing process.

Instructions:

- Quiet self-reflection: Get yourself to a peaceful, comfortable spot where you can think deeply and clearly without interruptions.
- Identify personal shadows: Consider aspects of yourself that you may have deemed unacceptable or kept hidden away. These could be traits, emotions, or memories that evoke discomfort.
- Write a shadow journal: Create a shadow journal in which you candidly write about these aspects. Explore the origins of these shadows and the role they play in your life.
- Reflect on impact: Consider how these shadows have influenced your behavior, relationships, and self-perception. Reflect on whether they stem from societal influences, childhood experiences, or other sources.
- Practice self-compassion: As you delve into your shadows, practice self-compassion. You can aid your recovery by accepting and even celebrating these characteristics, which are inherent to being human.

- Visual representation: Optionally, create a visual representation of your shadows using drawings, symbols, or colors. This can provide a tangible representation of the work you are doing.

Shadow Work: mending your wounded self

We all have demons. We battle them every day: sometimes, we succeed, and some others we fail. We may catch fleeting glimpses of these demons haunting us, or we may witness complete anarchy. We also tend to suppress and overlook them due to our shame and guilt.

We believe that they ought to remain hidden as they are incompatible with us and belong outside of our conscious selves. It's a societal norm to emphasize the positive aspects of life, such as love and light, rather than dwell on negativity or shadows.

Concentrating only on your positive traits is easy and cozy. It makes sense that most of us try to stay away from our darker sides.

But if we only pay attention to what's on the surface, it doesn't pierce the core of who we are. It's like clutching on to something warm and fluffy on the surface. There are deeper issues that every one of us has to deal with. We must be willing to use shadow work to examine our buried selves in order to reach the very core of who we are.

And rather than suppressing our darker sides, we must connect with them in order to find true serenity. Below are the fundamentals of shadow work that you should be aware of.

First, we must clarify what a "shadow" is.

In psychological terms, the shadow refers to the parts of ourselves that we would prefer to keep hidden or reject. The word was first used by Carl Jung, a Swiss physician and psychologist.

It consists of the aspects of our personalities that we often find repulsive, unattractive, or embarrassing. Envy, jealousy, fury, passion, a thirst for control, or childhood wounds are just a few examples of the emotions we hide.

You may call it a person's dark side. However, contrary to popular belief, every single person has a shadow side. According to Jung, the human shadow tends to undermine our life when it is rejected. Suppressing or repressing one's shadow can lead to a variety of neuroses, addictions, mental diseases, low self-esteem, and chronic illnesses.

Contrary to what you may be telling yourself at the moment, not all is lost. To accomplish your goals and lead the greatest possible life, you can learn to recognize and engage with your shadow self.

For many individuals, the path that they normally pick is to deny their inner self, but as you'll see here, I am in big favor of rather recognizing who you truly are and working with that while choosing deliberate thoughts and emotions to help you move forward.

The kind of transformation that so many of us seek doesn't originate in denial. It's the result of acceptance. Fortunately, we still have the ability to face our darkness and bring about constructive change. Shadow work allows us to expose our shadow selves rather than projecting a persona entirely in the light.

I'm here to inform you that, despite your doubts, it is possible to journey to the dark side of yourself and emerge a better person. In truth, you might benefit more if you accept what you believe is preventing you from moving forward. Included here are eight strategies to help you take control of your shadow self and live the life that was intended for you.

1. Have faith that things will improve and that you deserve it

Recognizing that you deserve nice things in life is the first step toward conquering your shadow self. It's easy to stay depressed while we're feeling that way. People have a remarkable capacity for self-pity, and occasionally, that is all we want to do.

However, there are moments when self-pity consumes us and makes it extremely difficult for us to break free of the pattern and return to our regular selves or, even better, our best selves. The secret is to develop self-love.

2. Identify the shadow

Our shadows reside in our subconscious. Because we buried them there, it's difficult to identify them.

We must identify the shadow in order to carry out shadow work. The first step is to recognize the feelings that come back to you time and time again. Finding these patterns will help in drawing attention to the shadow.

Some of the beliefs originating from the shadow include things like:

- I'm unlovable.
- I'm not good enough.
- I'm flawed.
- I have to look out for everyone around me.
- My feelings are invalid.
- Why can't I just be like everyone else?

3. Be mindful of the feelings you experience.

Emotions are all good. Our bad feelings serve as entryways into the shadow. They help us identify our scars and anxieties. Spend a moment analyzing each emotion you experience. Before you do anything, consider these questions:

- How am I feeling on the inside?
- What's causing my current emotional state?

Do your best not to lose your cool if you don't immediately know the answers. Sometimes, it takes time to find them, but you'll know when you do.

Never impose your will on others or draw hasty conclusions since they might not be right. Shadow work has its own schedule and is regarded as soul work. Just have patience and trust that the answers will become clear eventually. At this point, all it takes is to acknowledge that you are an emotional human who, from time to time, may have trouble controlling your emotions and embracing them as they arise.

4. Look into your feelings compassionately and objectively.

It's challenging to perform shadow work compassionately and objectively. It's easier to look around and pin the responsibility for your situation on other people.

However, it can be difficult to accept why the people who hurt you behaved in the ways they did. However, forgiving others who have harmed us is essential if we are to move on and recover. Consider the possibility that they were merely acting out of their own hurt or that they did the best they could at that moment.

It's also easy to beat yourself up over these negative feelings. However, there's no cause for alarm. Everybody feels bad sometimes. If we didn't, we wouldn't be human. It's critical to acknowledge and embrace our unpleasant feelings.

5. Paying attention to your breathing

To what extent do you observe your breathing patterns? Not a lot, if you're like most people. Usually, we just let our bodies take care of things and forget about them entirely.

This is, in my opinion, one of our worst mistakes since breathing generates energy for both your body and mind. Your heart, muscles, neurological system, brain, digestion, sleep, and mood are all directly impacted by this.

The way you breathe has a significantly greater influence on the quality of your breathing than the air itself. This is why breathing is such an important aspect of many spiritual systems. The practice of breathing awareness is one important tool employed to help individuals in exploring and ultimately conquer their shadow selves.

6. Explore the shadow

Art therapy is a tool used by psychologists to help patients discover more about themselves. That's because creating art is a wonderful way to let your shadow come to life. Below are some ways to express the shadow:

- **Writing a journal**

    You can experience emotions and clear your mind of stray thoughts while you write. It works like magic, even when you write nonsensical thoughts. Don't worry about making mistakes — just jot down whatever comes to mind.

- **Meditating**

    We become more aware of the reasons behind our feelings when we meditate. It supports us in understanding and objectively delving deeper into our feelings so that we can finally let them go and heal. Forgiveness meditation is one example. You can imagine someone who has wronged you and wish them happiness, serenity, and an end to their suffering.

- **Feeling**

    If you don't let yourself experience the feeling you're afraid of, you'll never be able to heal. Thus, explore them, write about them, and use them to inspire creativity. You must accept your feelings if you want to feel complete, appreciated, and likable.

- **Dreams**

Dreams are where our innermost feelings and ideas might surface. As soon as you have a dream, write it down and keep a record so you won't forget it. You may learn more about yourself by analyzing your dreams. However, it's crucial to realize that while a single dream might not signify anything, patterns from several dreams might.

Keep in mind that while the shadow exists in secret, it's still an integral part of who you are. Accept and love the pieces of yourself that are concealed, then bring them to the surface. Although the process can be painful at times, it will improve you as a person.

In order to succeed, you need to confront and maybe even embrace your shadow side. Instead of attempting to stifle your shadow, accept it and find fascination in it when it rears its ugly head.

Sometimes, you may find that it benefits you, particularly if you are trying to defend against something that could otherwise pose harm to your higher self.

When you know how to use your shadow self, it can be a strong change in your ego that supports you through difficult times. Problems arise when you allow it to control your life or act as though you don't have a shadow self.

7. Nurture your inner child

Our upbringing or other individuals who have harmed us may have contributed to our childhood traumas. Deep scars may arise from it, and those wounds may give birth to emotional and behavioral patterns that shape our personalities.

We tend to carry the scars from our childhoods with us to this day. They follow us, telling us we're unworthy of love, that our emotions are misguided, or that we must take care of ourselves because no one else did. Traveling back in time to a period when you were harmed and showing yourself love is part of tending to your inner child. To accomplish this, you can:

- **Recall the period of your life when you were most vulnerable**

It could be an incident in which you were harmed or a time when you experienced vulnerability. Keep that mental picture of yourself. Keep your eyes open and listen for any messages that come up.

- **Show compassion to your younger self**

  Give love to your younger self while you relive the occasion. Simply reminding yourself that you have your support says a lot. You did nothing to deserve this, so it's not your fault, and everything will work out. You might even hug your younger self.

There's no denying that shadow work is, to put it mildly, uncomfortable. Who would be happy admitting their shortcomings, self-centeredness, hatred, and all other unpleasant feelings they have experienced? No one.

Though it's fun and increases our self-esteem to concentrate on our positive traits, shadow work can actually help us become better versions of ourselves. We grow whole through shadow work and lead more genuine and satisfying lives.

Exercise: "Integration and Healing Ritual"
Description: After exploring your shadow self, engage in a healing ritual to integrate and reconcile with these aspects. This exercise fosters a sense of acceptance and wholeness, allowing you to move forward in your inner child healing journey with a more integrated and balanced self.

Instructions:

- Select a Symbolic Item: Choose a symbolic item that represents your commitment to integration and healing. Anything with sentimental value might do, such as a keepsake, an heirloom item, or a piece of jewelry.
- Create a Sacred Space: Get yourself to a peaceful, comfy spot where you won't be interrupted. Put the selected object in the middle.

- Acknowledgment and Acceptance: Take a few moments to acknowledge and accept the shadows you've explored. Recognize them as parts of yourself that deserve understanding and integration.

- Speak Your Intentions: Verbally express your intentions for healing and integration. Speak aloud your commitment to embracing all aspects of yourself, shadows included.

- Place the Item in your Journal: If you've created a journal, place the symbolic item within its pages as a representation of your ongoing commitment to integration.

- Visualization and Meditation: Imagine, with your eyes closed, how light and shadow become one with you. Meditate on the sense of wholeness and acceptance. Imagine a warm light enveloping your entire being.

- Express Gratitude: At the end of the ritual, you should be thankful for the chance to learn and heal. Thank yourself for the courage to undertake this important aspect of your inner child healing journey.

CHAPTER FIVE

CBT TECHNIQUES FOR HEALING

Picture yourself when you were younger, with all your aspirations, anxieties, and life events that have shaped who you are now. As we saw in the previous chapters, this version of yourself is your inner child and not just a memory. Setting out on a quest to discover, treat, and develop this inner child can be a life-changing experience that results in increased self-worth, personal growth, and a happier, healthier version of yourself.

In the journey of inner child healing, Cognitive Behavioral Therapy (CBT) emerges as a transformative ally, providing a structured and effective framework for introspection and growth. CBT, rooted in the principles of identifying and challenging negative thought patterns, plays a crucial role in unraveling the intricacies of our inner child wounds.

At the core of CBT lies the exploration of automatic negative thoughts, many of which find their roots in formative childhood experiences. By bringing these thoughts to the light, individuals engaging in CBT embark on a path of self-discovery, unraveling the layers that shroud their inner child. This process involves understanding the core beliefs that were shaped during childhood, beliefs that continue to influence perceptions and reactions.

The heart of the CBT contribution to inner child healing lies in its ability to restructure cognition. Individuals develop a more grounded and practical outlook through therapy procedures and guided reflection that teaches them to confront and recast erroneous ideas. This cognitive restructuring directly addresses thought patterns that may have originated in the formative years, providing a platform for healing.

CBT embraces behavioral experiments and exposure exercises to further reinforce its role in the healing journey. Controlled exposure to thoughts and situations associated with past traumas becomes a methodical step toward desensitization and, ultimately, healing. The therapeutic approach of CBT not only encourages individuals to confront their shadows but also guides them through a process of acceptance and transformation.

As individuals progress through CBT, they are equipped with practical coping strategies tailored to manage distressing emotions and navigate triggers linked to inner child wounds. The development of these coping skills fosters emotional regulation, providing individuals with tools to confront challenges from a place of resilience and self-awareness.

During inner child healing, CBT operates as more than just a therapeutic technique: it becomes a facilitator of self-compassion. Cognitive Behavioral Therapy teaches people to be more compassionate and understanding toward themselves by addressing negative self-talk. This shift in internal dialogue becomes essential in countering the negative messages internalized during childhood, laying the foundation for a more compassionate relationship with one's inner child.

Ultimately, the integration of CBT in the inner child healing process unveils a profound connection between the therapeutic approach and the journey toward wholeness. By addressing cognitive distortions, exploring core beliefs, and fostering coping strategies, CBT becomes a guiding light in the transformative process of acknowledging, healing, and embracing the inner child.

Cognitive behavioral therapy

CBT has been the most widely studied and recognized form of psychotherapy. It combines two distinct approaches: behavioral therapy and cognitive therapy. The illness or issue that has to be treated determines which therapy techniques are used. Nonetheless, the fundamental idea guiding treatment remains constant: our thoughts, feelings, and behaviors are all intimately related, and they all have a significant impact on our overall well-being.

What is cognitive therapy?

The word cognitive originates from *Cognoscere*, a Latin word that means "to recognize." In cognitive therapy, the focus is helping the patient gain insight into their own thought processes, values, and expectations. The goal is to expose and dispel untrue and upsetting beliefs because, more often than not, it's our attachment to things and circumstances that lead to problems.

One potentially harmful thought pattern is, for example, when someone quickly draws negative conclusions from one incident and applies them to other similar circumstances. This broad-minded approach to thinking is known as over-generalizing in psychology. Having a catastrophic and pessimistic approach is another unsettling error in our reasoning: when anything unsettling occurs, some individuals instantly draw exaggerated conclusions about the alleged impending catastrophe.

These kinds of thought patterns can occasionally become self-fulfilling prophecies, which negatively impact the affected individuals' quality of life. Cognitive therapy teaches people how to swap out these negative thought patterns for more sensible and constructive ones. Additionally, it improves one's ability to think more clearly and effectively.

How does CBT help inner child healing?

Cognitive behavioral therapy offers several advantages over other types of therapy for healing your inner child. Some of them are shown here:

1. Gaining insight into emotions and ideas

CBT helps you understand why you feel the way you do. It's like illuminating your innermost sensations and ideas so you can trace their origins. This is important for inner child healing because it helps you connect with the little you inside — the part of you that holds onto feelings from when you were young.

2. Changing negative thoughts

CBT lets you know how to change negative thoughts. Imagine if you often feel not good enough or scared. CBT shows you how to challenge these thoughts and exchange them with more positive and realistic ones. This is like rewriting the script in your mind that was written during your childhood.

3. Dealing with bad memories

If there are memories from when you were a child that make you feel sad or upset, CBT helps you deal with them. It's like having a guide who helps you face those memories bit by bit, making them less scary and more manageable.

4. Learning better ways to cope

Sometimes, when we feel overwhelmed, we don't know how to cope. CBT teaches us practical ways to handle tough situations. It's like having a toolkit with strategies that help you stay calm and feel stronger, especially when old feelings pop up.

5. Connecting past and present

CBT shows you how your past experiences can still affect you today. It's like connecting the dots between what happened when you were little and how you react to things now. Understanding this link is key to healing your inner child.

6. Facing fears gradually

If there are things that scare you because of what happened in the past, CBT helps you face them slowly. It's like taking small steps to overcome fears, making them less powerful over time. This is crucial for healing because it allows you to feel more in control.

7. Building confidence and self-compassion

CBT boosts your confidence by challenging self-doubt. It's like having a cheerleader in your mind, reminding you that you are worthy and capable. When you practice self-compassion, you can help your inner child recover from the hurts they may have experienced.

8. Creating a positive inner dialogue

CBT helps change the way you talk to yourself in your mind. It's like switching from a harsh critic to a supportive friend. This shift in your inner dialogue is essential for healing, as it nurtures a kinder relationship with your inner child.

9. Setting Small Goals for Progress

CBT encourages you to set small, achievable goals. It's like taking one step at a time toward feeling better. These goals become milestones on your healing journey, showing you that progress is happening.

10. Building a Stronger You

Ultimately, CBT helps you build a stronger and more resilient version of yourself. It's like constructing a sturdy foundation for your emotional well-being. This resilience will carry you through the process of healing your inner child and advancing in life.

CBT is like a helpful guide that walks you through the process of understanding, facing, and healing the emotions of your inner child. It provides practical tools and a positive mindset, empowering you to take control of your healing journey step by step.

Techniques for healing your inner child

Starting the process of healing your inner child with Cognitive Behavioral Therapy offers you access to a wide range of therapeutic approaches, each of which has a unique role in the complex process of self-awareness and recovery.

- **Somatic experiencing**

Conceive somatic experiencing methods as a way to communicate with your body and the feelings of your inner child. Observe any physical reactions that come up when you recall the past. Through gentle movement, shaking, or grounding techniques, let any feelings come to the surface and be expressed. This can facilitate healing by releasing pent-up tension.

- **Self-Compassion meditations**

Meditate with self-compassion, addressing your inner child head-on. Close your eyes, put your hands over your heart, and talk to yourself as though you were talking to your inner child. The following statements could help validate their needs and emotions: "It's understandable that you feel sad," "Right now, you're safe," or "You deserve love and understanding." Treat your inner child with the same compassion and consolation that you would use with a crying infant.

- **Grounding techniques**

Incorporate grounding strategies when working with your inner child. In order to feel safe and rooted in your here and now, try sensory-focused activities. Find something to hold onto, focus on your breathing, or just observe the sensation of your feet touching the floor.

- **Mindfulness techniques**

Engage in mindfulness exercises to develop self-awareness and witness your inner child's experiences without passing judgment. Establish a safe zone inside yourself where you can observe and accept the feelings and memories that resurface. As you give in to these feelings, keep in mind that you are here in the here and now, free from the chains of the past.

- **Chair work exercises**

Chair work is a powerful tool for healing the inner child. Arrange a pair of seats and imagine your adult self-sitting on one while your inner child occupies the other. Talk back and forth between the two, letting your inner child share their needs, desires, and feelings. As an adult, give consolation, assurance, and direction; give your inner child the love and support it might not have received.

- **Reparenting visualizations**

Reparenting visualizations and guided imagery are useful tools for healing and nurturing your inner child. Picture your grown-up self-entering previous situations or traumatic experiences where your inner child was harmed or neglected. Defend your inner child by speaking up against harmful influences and providing the love, support, and affirmation that your inner child needs to hear in that particular moment.

- **Journaling and letter-writing**

Keeping a journal might help you reconnect with your younger self. Write letters expressing support, compassion, and empathy to your younger self. Offer consoling words, affirm their feelings, and acknowledge their grief. This procedure can promote integration and healing while enabling a closer relationship with your inner child.

Working with our inner child offers us the chance to investigate and understand the demands that were unfulfilled in our early years. Examining our past experiences might help us identify patterns of emotional deprivation, abandonment, or neglect that left us with unmet needs.

These unfulfilled wants might show up in our adult relationships, which can interfere with our capacity to establish healthy bonds and reasonable limits.

We adopt the role of a loving caregiver to our inner child when we engage in inner child work. As we develop sensitivity to their emotions and needs, we learn to hear them out and react compassionately. The process of healing and repair starts when we recognize and validate these needs.

Effective communication techniques support the healing of childhood trauma and enable us to manage our own needs in adult relationships. It entails establishing clear boundaries, demands, and wants in the relationships we are in right now. This could be stating our preferences, putting boundaries in place, or asking for help. We actively seek to satisfy the needs of our inner children and foster a healing atmosphere by speaking up for their demands.

Exercise: Specific Cognitive Behavioral Therapy Techniques for Inner Child Healing

Description: This exercise is designed to help you explore and understand the origins of certain beliefs or behaviors rooted in your childhood experiences. By identifying these roots, you can begin the process of healing and transforming them.

Instructions:

- Reflection: Set aside dedicated time for self-reflection. Think about a specific negative belief or behavior pattern that you often encounter in your adult life. It could be related to self-worth, relationships, or any other aspect.

- Journaling: In your workbook, create a timeline of your life. Highlight key events or moments that might be connected to the identified belief or behavior. Reflect on your early experiences, family dynamics, and significant life events during your formative years.

- Connect the Dots: Analyze the connections between your current belief or behavior and the events from your past. Consider how your inner child might have interpreted those situations and formed certain beliefs as a result.

- Reframe and Rewrite: Challenge the negative beliefs by reframing them in a more positive or balanced light. Write a compassionate and empowering statement that counteracts the original belief. This new narrative should focus on self-love, acceptance, and understanding.

- Visualize Integration: Close your eyes and visualize your adult self-embracing and comforting your inner child. Imagine sharing the rewritten narrative with your inner child, fostering a sense of safety and reassurance.
- Journal Reflection: Write down your feelings, insights, and any emotions that surfaced during this exercise. Acknowledge the progress you've made and the compassion you've shown to your inner child.

Identifying and addressing dysfunctional thoughts and behaviors

You most likely feel more grounded in your emotions and aren't as easily taken away by them now that you know how to monitor your mood and recognize automatic thoughts. The focus of this section is to help you create significant shifts in your beliefs, emotions, and actions from that new, stable position.

Here, we will be honing a skill known as cognitive restructuring. Cognitive restructuring is the process of recognizing inefficient thought patterns and changing them to become more effective. Being more effective can entail triggering fewer negative feelings, improving clarity of vision, or facilitating more skillful behaviors. Cognitive restructuring builds on your capacity to notice automatic thoughts and sensations with accuracy.

When people hear about cognitive restructuring, they often associate it with the idea of positive thinking — the notion that pleasure can be attained by seeing bad circumstances in a good light. In truth, extreme positivism and extreme negativism can both be equally ineffective. If you are worried that you won't do well on the first date, the date may definitely go badly. However, supposing that, for example, a date would go well no matter what could make you less worried about how you behave with your date, which could potentially lead to a bad date.

It's not necessary to be overly optimistic when implementing cognitive restructuring. That's referred to as denial, and it's not a very useful coping mechanism. The goal of cognitive restructuring is to create a more nuanced worldview that considers both positive and negative viewpoints. As a result, you will be able to adopt a mindset that will help you accomplish your goals more successfully and will cause you to feel less unpleasant feeling.

Sometimes, after restructuring a dysfunctional thought, you may experience an instantaneous positive mood shift. In other cases, you might need to practice a different perspective on a difficult circumstance before it begins to register in your mind and affect your emotions. The key to cognitive restructuring is consistent practice until it becomes second nature and doesn't require additional effort from you.

Coming up with alternatives

Cognitive restructuring enables individuals to view their experiences from fresh perspectives. Part of the practice involves creating logical and constructive replacements for the distorted explanations that have been accepted over time.

For instance, rather than concluding that you're bad at math if you didn't do as well on a test, consider how you can improve your study techniques. Alternatively, you might research some relaxing ways to exercise before your upcoming exam.

Here's another example: if a group of coworkers stops talking when you enter a room, you might want to think about other possible reasons for their behavior before assuming that they were talking negatively about you. By doing this, you can realize that you were misinterpreting the circumstance or that it had nothing to do with you.

Creating uplifting affirmations and substituting logical thought patterns for false or detrimental ones are two great methods of generating alternatives.

You may want to tell yourself that you contribute positively and passionately at work and that your coworkers always include you in discussions. These affirmations can be based on a list of the real contributions you've made and the beneficial connections you've formed.

Writing down your daily thoughts allows you to understand which ones repeat the most and shows you the patterns you have. Another way is to neutrally observe the results and actions you perform to evaluate the inner pattern that made you perform them. These processes allow you to become aware of yourself. As soon as you notice a pattern or a negative situation, it's good to repeat the previous exercise.

Exercise: Challenging Dysfunctional Thoughts and Behaviors

Description: This exercise utilizes Cognitive Behavioral Therapy techniques to help you recognize and challenge dysfunctional thoughts and behaviors linked to your inner child's wounds. By interrupting negative patterns, you pave the way for positive change.

Instructions:

- Awareness Journal: Begin by creating an Awareness Journal section in your workbook. List recurring negative thoughts and behaviors that hinder your personal growth and well-being.

- Identify Cognitive Distortions: Look over your list and see if any of the typical cognitive distortions, like negative assumptions, catastrophizing, or detrimental thinking, pop up. Write down the distorted thought patterns associated with each negative belief or behavior.

- Reality Check: For each distorted thought, challenge its validity. Ask yourself if there is evidence supporting or contradicting the thought. Consider alternatives or more balanced perspectives.

- Construct Affirmations: Develop positive affirmations that counteract dysfunctional thoughts. Focus on statements that promote self-compassion, resilience, and personal growth.

- Behavioral Activation: Choose one dysfunctional behavior to address. Break it down into smaller, manageable phases that align with your new affirmations. Gradually incorporate positive changes into your routine.

- Track Progress: Create a tracking system in your workbook to monitor your progress. Regularly revisit and update your Awareness Journal, noting any shifts in your thoughts, feelings, and behaviors.

CHAPTER SIX

ACCEPTANCE AND INTEGRATION

At the beginning of existence, both light and shadow were created at the same time. The radiant energy of light opposes its counterpart, the shadow. However, what exactly is a shadow? It is the actual deformation or distortion of light. We must acknowledge the shadows that the light casts to fully use its potential. Therefore, we must set out on a path of healing from our past, both our own and that of our lineage, in order to shape our future.

First of all, we must face and accept our own shadow in order to develop self-awareness and love for everything that has been and ever will be. By doing this, we become more fully ourselves and turn darkness into light, that is, bringing our dark and unaccepted sides to a higher level of awareness and acceptance.

Healing processes never end because we always move forward and leave the past behind. Because the past (and the darkness) will always coexist with the future, humanity will never be able to exclaim, "Ah, I have completely emerged into the light of consciousness and myself!" The secret is to find peace in each stride we've taken and to let the light shine on us. Healing, therefore, is looking into the past, understanding what happened, and bringing it to a higher level of awareness.

In addition to using meditation, those who awaken their consciousness often do so in reaction to a serious crisis. Respecting the crisis that ignites our awakening allows our awareness to withstand and penetrate all aspects of existence. Identifying our shadow turns into a crucial part of this process.

We can change who we are now by keeping track of the past, appreciating it for what it was, and reflecting on it. Forgiveness is a great tool that can change our entire path, just as it can change the way we see the future. It's by acknowledging the unpleasant experiences and, at times, grieving them, that we back the feelings (and their energies) that were solidified before. We enable these energies to flow freely within us by removing their stagnation. Through this process, we discover our potential, gain insight, and express gratitude for the transforming journey that advances our growth by transforming darkness into light and our pain into calm.

A strong foundation in the past is essential for building the future. Denying the past and its shadow results in a never-ending circle of stagnation. We admit that when we were younger or in other situations, we lacked the knowledge and resources necessary to properly grasp our past. However, we can change our viewpoint and strengthen our future by forgiving.

Acceptance of the past and the shadow

It can be difficult to accept the past and move on with your recovery. You may have had trauma in the past, which continues to influence your day-to-day existence. You can be terrified to make changes or concerned about potential outcomes. Trauma causes your mind to start seeing things differently. You could not be accepting of what had transpired or its consequences. You might be finding it difficult to embrace your trauma because of its complexity and the reason behind it. After all, as a victim, how are you going to come to terms with what went down?

Letting go and moving on might depend on your ability to accept the past. That horrible experience you had wasn't your fault. You have nothing to blame for the events that occurred to you. Saying that things weren't that horrible or that they didn't damage you could cause you to argue with yourself. Your refusal to embrace your past is reflected in this denial. You might need to accept your past — good or bad — in order to move on from your trauma, regardless of the circumstances that led to it. You may reconstruct your life beyond your trauma by overcoming the pain. Healing can start when you accept the past and move on. You can have the best possible life, and the healing process includes acceptance. Remember this while you navigate the challenging road to recovery. The challenge is worth it!

It could be necessary for you to have some perspective on the past and realize that you can change the course of your future. It's possible that a lot of unpleasant events in your past have left you feeling powerless over your future. You might think that your terrible feelings won't go away or that you'll never be able to get over tragic events. Recovery is a lifelong struggle, and you can go on by getting over your pain.

Although other mental strength exercises can help you let go of the past, the following two strategies are particularly efficient for you to move forward.

1. Accept the past as it is

It could take some time for you to consider the reasons why you're stuck in the past. Do you think you're not worthy of moving forward? Perhaps you believe that remaining in the past is your punishment for hurting someone.

Do you believe that your anger makes someone else's life less valuable? And thus, you're holding onto a grudge? Perhaps you're concerned that if you move on from someone who hurt you, it won't prove that what they did was all that horrible.

Sometimes, it's easy to divert your attention from the present by thinking about the past. A person who is now miserable could find it easy to fantasize about how much better life was back then. Maybe you think back to all the wonderful things that happened in a past relationship, and you ignore all the conflicts and issues that caused the relationship to end.

The truth is that you can never tell what the future holds based on the decisions you made in the past. Perhaps you even blame yourself for having made a single wrong choice. Depending on your situation, you might only need to allow yourself to move on and then deliberately try to force yourself to stop thinking about the past each time you find yourself stuck.

Have you experienced trauma and neglected your need for help? You might benefit from professional help to heal that old emotional wound if a terrible or traumatic occurrence is what is keeping you stuck in the past. You might be able to move on for good by having a conversation with a qualified mental health expert.

2. Pay attention to what you have learned

You'll stay trapped if you focus on how unfair or terrible an incident was. You might need to take some time to focus on the facts rather than the feelings in order to heal.

Take a moment to revisit a distressing memory and focus on the details rather than your emotions. Recall who was with you, where you were, what you were doing, and what happened to you. Then, think back to the lessons you learned from getting through that difficult situation or from surviving that awful thing. Your most difficult experiences can teach you some of the most valuable life lessons.

So, try going over the specifics as if you were a narrator who just tells the facts, whether you write in a notebook or retell the narrative in your head. Repeating this can help lessen the emotional impact of the experience.

Let go of the past, live now, and make plans for the future

Refusing to dwell on the past doesn't necessarily mean ignoring the past. Rather, it usually entails accepting and embracing your past to live in the present, thus acknowledging the emotional toll that obsessing over something is having on you and then allowing yourself to move on.

Forgiving someone who harmed you could be necessary in this situation. You might need to follow through with your decision to cut off communication with the person; this does not imply simply forgive and forget them. However, put your attention on forgivingness by letting go of your hurt or resentment toward them.

It's important to focus on who you want to become in the future rather than who you were in the past. Hence, while you can look back long enough to draw lessons from it, be sure to let go of any resentment, guilt, or shame that is preventing you from moving forward.

Exercise: Embracing the Past

Description: This exercise encourages a deeper exploration of your past experiences and the acceptance of the shadow aspects of your personality. By facing and embracing these elements, you create space for healing and integration.

Instructions:

- Mindful Reflection: Find a quiet and comfortable space for mindful reflection. Bring your attention to your breath and create a sense of inner calm. Acknowledge that this exercise is a safe space for exploring your past.

- Past Acceptance Journal: Open a new section in your workbook titled Past Acceptance Journal. Begin by jotting down any emotions, memories, or events from your past that may still carry emotional weight.

- Emotional Inquiry: Explore the emotions associated with these past experiences and shadow aspects. Allow yourself to feel without judgment. Recognize that these emotions are valid and part of your human experience.

- Symbolic Release: Consider a symbolic gesture of releasing the past. This could involve writing down burdensome memories on paper and ceremoniously burning or tearing them apart, symbolizing your willingness to let go.

- Integration Reflection: Reflect on how the process of acknowledging and accepting your past has influenced your current emotional state. Note any shifts in perception or feelings of liberation.

Integrating the shadow of the past into inner child healing

Here I'll introduce the idea of integration. Integration implies merging or combining. A person's various aspects can integrate into their whole when they undergo this process. It relies on the belief that in order to fully embrace your actual identity in life and relationships, you must first release and heal damaged portions of yourself. Integrating means being complete.

Accepting the painful parts

Your trauma needs to be resolved; it's not something you need to integrate. Instead, what needs to be integrated are the pieces of the human soul that the trauma has broken apart. The adult most commonly rejects, ignores, or shames the wounded child aspects of the self. The emotionally wounded portions of oneself must first be embraced by the core self for them to fully heal. Despite the difficulty, it's possible to overcome feelings of shame and humiliation by learning to accept and love yourself, flaws and all.

One practice that can help you forgive your child self is imagining a child you know who is the same age as you were when you were hurt. You can picture how hard it would be for a 9-year-old child to handle this, for instance, if they were going through a trauma comparable to yours. Typically, we are more critical of ourselves than we are of other people. Practicing empathy for your younger self could be as simple as putting yourself in their shoes for a while.

Healing requires accepting your younger self and not shaming them. It's also critical to acknowledge and accept the reactions that this damaged area currently elicits. Anger outbursts, addictions, self-loathing, and other issues are linked to current circumstances that relieve painful memories. It's crucial to calm yourself rather than criticize yourself when these reactions arise. This is effective because you can only change if you make an effort to embrace your most wounded and vulnerable aspects of yourself. Reassuring yourself with words, such as "I understand your response" could offer some relief. After what you've been through, it's understandable.

Once we cease to be hard on ourselves, we can begin to release our burdens. This process involves allowing the trauma to progress through the body and mind toward a resolution. It's time to give the younger parts of ourselves a chance to relax after this process has been completed.

Releasing the wounded parts to rest

The aftermath of trauma may make it more difficult for wounded areas to heal. The effects of trauma can be like a time machine for our bodies and thoughts. On the other hand, trauma may be resolved, and people can go on to have happy, fulfilled lives with time and intention.

Your actual identity, which is composed of stronger, more mature components, solidifies when the trauma is healed. Your younger self can heal with the help of these stronger, more experienced aspects of you. The wounded parts no longer need to be provoked and react in unhealthy or protective ways when the genuine identity is reinforced, and the hurt starts to heal. Now that you're more mature, you can decide when and how to react to certain circumstances. At last, the wounded self can rest.

Wounded experiences get imprinted or frozen in the psyche, preventing the real self from ever being able to emerge. Many people think that their immature reactions or vices are just part of who they are. There is no way that this is the case. The basis of immature reactions is pain. Healing from trauma and integrating aspects of oneself makes room for the real, more mature self to emerge reliably and consistently.

Forgiving one's younger self, realizing with compassion and accuracy because they reacted the way they did, and allowing them to rest and be at peace until the end of time are all wonderful experiences. Your younger self has endured a great deal while striving to protect you up until this point. They should be allowed to go to a place where your willing, competent, and responsible adult self can take care of them.

Walking lighter

Throughout this integration process, you'll experience both physical and mental changes. It's difficult to live with unresolved trauma. Putting forth the effort to heal and integrate yields lasting results in terms of both mental and physical health. Feeling lighter, freer, more capable, and more complete upon waking up one day is a strange sensation. Recognizing the full extent of the wound, confronting the anguish, and opening oneself up to new, healing relationships that fill the void left by the old ones are all parts of trauma therapy. The heaviness you tolerated and accepted as normal is now gone. A fresh life full of delight in relationships and optimism for the future has replaced it.

I have experience with this firsthand. Enjoying yourself and having the freedom to express yourself clearly and confidently feels amazing. It's time to change for the many of us who experienced trauma as children and haven't had an accurate identity mirrored back to us. It's crucial to surround yourself with like-minded people who are experiencing similar things in life and who share your ideals. Finding individuals who accept you for who you really are and who can confidently and accurately reflect your identity is crucial since you are not alone on this path.

The most difficult aspects of healing your inner child are admitting the hurt and giving the memories time to be processed. Integrating into this system is like finding a treasure trove of riches at the end of a rainbow. People who accept this challenge and endure the effort to heal are bestowed with optimism for the future, a fresh outlook, a healed heart, improved interpersonal skills, and a strong sense of self and the universe. My personal goal is for everyone to participate in this process. Even though I'm aware that not everyone will be able to handle life's hardships to this extent, my deepest desire is for every person to find forgiveness and healing. There are countless horrible crimes committed against children in this life. If we don't break this pattern, wounded children will grow up to hurt other children.

Adults who have experienced healing encourage healing and give the next generation courage. Together, we embody the qualities of maturity.

Exercise: Shadow Integration

Description: This exercise focuses on integrating the shadow aspects identified in the previous exercises into your inner child healing journey. By acknowledging and integrating these aspects, you promote a holistic approach to self-discovery and healing.

Instructions:

- Shadow Inventory: Review the list of shadow aspects you identified in the previous exercises. Choose one aspect to work on during this session.

- Compassionate Inquiry: Engage in a compassionate inner dialogue with the chosen shadow aspect. Ask questions such as: "What purpose did you serve in my past?" or "How can I integrate you into my present with love and understanding?"

- Creative Expression: Use a creative medium (drawing, writing, or even movement) to express the energy of the shadow aspect. Allow your inner child to participate in this expression, fostering a sense of collaboration.

- Positive Integration Affirmations: Develop positive affirmations that acknowledge the value of the integrated shadow aspect. Focus on how it can contribute to your personal growth, resilience, and self-awareness.

- Visualization: Close your eyes and visualize your integrated self, encompassing both light and shadow aspects. Imagine your inner child embracing and accepting this integrated version of yourself.

- Journal Reflection: Write about your experience with the integration process. Reflect on any insights gained, shifts in perspective, or feelings of empowerment. Note the positive qualities that have emerged through this integration.

- Future Integration Plan: Outline a plan for gradually integrating other shadow aspects into your inner child healing journey. Set realistic goals and milestones, recognizing that this process is ongoing.

Remember, the integration of shadow is a transformative and evolving process. Deal with it with patience and compassion toward yourself and be determined to cultivate every part of your genuine self.

CHAPTER SEVEN

BOUNDARIES, EMOTIONAL INTELLIGENCE, AND REPARENTING

An individual's inner child encompasses sources of resilience, humor, and/or skills acquired during their developmental phases. But it also includes wounds and traumas sustained during growth. It might take some time, but you can heal these wounds from your inner child.

This chapter invites us into a journey in which we'll explore three important things: boundaries, emotional intelligence, and reparenting. We'll start by learning how to set healthy boundaries, which are like invisible lines that help us take care of ourselves. Then, we'll dive into emotional intelligence, understanding and managing our feelings better. Finally, we'll discover the powerful practice of reparenting, a way of caring for ourselves like a loving parent.

This chapter is like a guide to becoming stronger, wiser, and more connected with the part of us that needs extra love and care.

Playful boundary-setting for personal growth

We often enjoy, as adults, having the independence to choose for ourselves without parental direction. But we all have a secret part of us that yearns for structure and the security it offers.

Becoming a responsible and loving parent and establishing and enforcing boundaries in a compassionate, firm, and nurturing way is all part of healing our inner child.

We fill in any developmental gaps we may have had when we become our own loving adult guardians. By doing this, we can awaken our creativity and vitality, allowing us to truly live and transform the worlds we live in.

Creating a sense of safety

- "Good morning; it's time to get up."
- "All right, let's tidy up now so we can leave!"
- "It's bedtime! Do not forget to brush your teeth!"

Our adult guardians were very important in providing boundaries, structure, and rules when we were kids. These boundaries establish constancy, dependability, and a sense of kinship with life's cycles, which eventually cultivates a sense of security. We have the chance to adopt this position as adults and provide our inner child with stability and comfort.

We create a framework where our inner child can flourish by establishing boundaries. Having this safety zone gives us more stability as we manage the difficulties of life.

The power of boundaries

The benefits of being an adult are numerous! Our time, effort, and focus are ours to control. Nobody has the right to control us. We get to make the rules!

Having rules and not having any rules at all are not the same thing. We are freed from the limitations imposed by an external authority as adults. This doesn't imply that there should be no rules at all! It can be alluring to have complete freedom.

We might like having the freedom to eat and speak as we please, sleep as we please, and spend our lives as we see fit. But even with this independence, there may be a lurking unhappiness. Quietly, our inner child reminds us of its needs —structure and direction.

You can get unsatisfied if you spend hours scrolling through Instagram. If you put off tasks and responsibilities, you can start hearing from your inner critic. This Guide may be bringing up the promises that you made to yourself. When this happens, inhale deeply and slowly and listen in. We keep laying the groundwork for our own development by accepting the boundaries we naturally establish for ourselves.

Nurturing the inner child

We often witness the results of damaged children growing up to be adults. Some people put on a hard façade and transfer their pain to others. For adults, discovering their inner child is a necessary and empowering experience. It entails treating ourselves as if we were our own responsible, loving parents and choosing more loving decisions that benefit both us and other people.

We can create boundaries for our inner child in the same way that a loving parent would for the sake of their child. Instead of using severe discipline or punishment, it's imperative to approach this process with kindness, firmness, and love.

The goal is to establish a space where our inner child feels loved, cared for, and safe. Talk to yourself more compassionately. Even if, at first, it seems strange or absurd. With practice, the inner voice starts to align with this more optimistic mindset. The kind remarks start to seem more real. This love seeps into the worlds you build.

Finding freedom despite limitations

Although setting boundaries may seem restrictive at first, it's crucial to realize how much joy and security they may bring. A crucial component of setting and upholding boundaries with our inner children is playfulness. Boundaries don't need to be always strict; sometimes, they serve as the structure for an enjoyable game of self-discovery.

Occasionally, we become aware of a boundary breach only after it has already occurred. Maybe you work so hard at your job that you forget to eat lunch, which has an impact on how you interact with others and how the rest of the day goes. After looking back on your day, you see that you overworked and put your own well-being in second place, in favor of a desired outcome. You acknowledge that you've gone too far.

Use this as a chance to affirm who you are. Establish a new boundary for yourself by setting an alert for the following day. Evaluate the circumstances, decide whether to change, and establish the guidelines. This gives you a sense of security that both your inner child and your outer adult enjoy.

Embracing transformation

Setting boundaries with our inner child is a self-care and development exercise. It enables us to give them the love, stability, and structure that they so much need. We create an atmosphere that supports our true selves and releases our creativity and energy when we take on this responsibility in a sincere and lighthearted way.

We not only get to experience life to the fullest through this life-changing journey, but we also have the ability to positively impact both our own lives and the lives of those around us.

Exercise: Boundaries Reinforcement

Description: This exercise is designed to help you identify, communicate, and reinforce healthy boundaries in your relationships. If you want to keep your emotional health and build better relationships with other people, setting boundaries is a must.

Instructions:

- Boundary Assessment: Take stock of your personal and professional connections as they stand right now. Recognize situations where you feel your boundaries are being challenged or crossed. Note these instances in your workbook.

- Clarifying Personal Values: List your core values and priorities. This will serve as a basis for establishing boundaries aligned with your authentic self.

- Boundary Setting Practice: Pick a relationship where you would benefit from setting or reiterating certain boundaries. Clearly define your boundaries in specific terms, expressing your needs and expectations.

- Communication Exercise: Practice communicating your boundaries assertively and respectfully. As a means of bolstering self-assurance, this may entail practicing hypothetical situations with a reliable friend or therapist.

- Consistent Reinforcement: Consistently reinforce your boundaries. Pay attention to your feelings and communicate any adjustments or changes to your boundaries as needed. Update your workbook with reflections on the outcomes.

- Self-Care Integration: Connect the practice of setting boundaries with self-care. Recognize that boundaries are an essential aspect of self-love and protection. Register self-care activities that support your overall well-being.

- Reflection and Adjustment: Periodically reflect on the impact of established boundaries on your relationships and emotional well-being. Adjust boundaries as necessary, emphasizing the importance of personal growth and evolving needs.

Emotional intelligence and the inner child

Here, I'd like to talk a little bit about what we think of as emotional intelligence and how it relates to inner child work.

The focus of inner child work is on triggering patterns of behavior. Imagine that you are with a child who could throw a tantrum at any time for any cause. We all have an element of this within us, and we can control the intensity of this reaction by practicing self-awareness or paying attention, which enables us to accept even bigger processes. These triggering elements then suggest that a root cause should be taken into account, and we monitor the actions to understand and address them.

We can interpret and negotiate our behavioral patterns, triggers, and emotions as we develop a trusting relationship with our inner child. When they feel that they are both responsible for their own safety and treated with respect, they behave better overall. This change in the connection gives us thoughts on how to reach a middle ground. When your inner child is given the respect they deserve, they can make suggestions about things they would want to accomplish and start talking more freely. They beseech you to remember that your happiness is only their delight.

Our mental activity changes as a result of this transition into emotional awareness. We are now actively monitoring our behavior from an impartial standpoint, and this change in mental pattern starts to introduce a different viewpoint regarding our self-perception and emotional beliefs. As it turns out, the inner child dislikes when we lie to ourselves. Our justifications and accommodations, which serve as both white lies to ourselves and serious breaches of our integrity, hinder our ability to evolve as individuals. Now that we have a fresh viewpoint let's start thinking about some of the signs of emotional immaturity:

- Emotional instability, which includes vulnerability, emotional outbursts, anger, anxiety over external factors, and inability to manage problems.
- Emotional regression: demotivation, self-doubt, inferiority complex, and unrest in the mind.
- Social maladjustment, which refers to a lack of social flexibility, social avoidance, and a reliance on justifications for social isolation.
- Disintegration of personality: erratic behavior, emergence of phobias, extreme pessimism.
- Lack of independence: reliance on others as a result of emotional manipulations.

Understanding the causes of behavioral symptoms becomes easier when we start to watch them objectively, that is, from outside of ourselves. From this point of view, we can start to understand the actions involved in increasing our emotional maturity:

- Emotional understanding and control
- Emotional honesty and openness
- Basic emotional responsibility
- Emotional detachment

Bring in the inner child

Creativity is required, and many people struggle to convey these feelings with a serious undertone. This is the wonderful part of working with the inner child. The change itself comes from the joy and kindness in the empathetic connection with our inner child; a lack of involvement and interest won't allow us to move intellectually.

You can see the fierce resistance that is stifling creativity when you urge a friend who is upset or furious to sing, dance, or just clap everything negative out of their thoughts. If you are successful, you'll witness a remarkable shift since the creative expression will quickly release any pent-up anger.

Most people resort to inner child work to deal with emotional outbursts, emotional hijacking, undermining, and harmful habits that have surfaced in their lives. We can quickly start to understand the sources and reasons behind these feelings, and if we can see that the response isn't justified by the trigger, that's when we can start to follow the threads and find the programming that sets us up for this particular behavioral outcome.

Since it requires a high level of emotional intelligence to see that change is necessary, entering this field with a serious approach usually pays off. You are prepared to tackle the theory and practice that will help you along the change path when you recognize that something needs to change. After the approach has been presented and you have the tools, it's up to you to decide when you are ready to assume accountability for your own actions.

Elevating your emotional intelligence in 9 simple steps

If you want to be more emotionally intelligent in the workplace or anywhere else, follow these steps:

1. Increase your self-awareness

Being aware of one's emotional reactions to those around can greatly enhance emotional intelligence. Being self-aware can help you deal with and express negative emotions (such as anger or anxiety) in a healthy way. If you wish to develop greater self-awareness, try writing down the circumstances around any intense emotional experience you have.

2. Acknowledge the feelings of others

While self-reflection is a great place to start when developing emotional intelligence, it's equally critical to consider how other people see your actions and interactions. Being emotionally savvy includes being able to change your message according to how you're perceived. To demonstrate that you value other people's opinions, you may always ask them how they feel if you're not sure.

3. Engage in active listening

People communicate both verbally and nonverbally, so it's critical to pay attention and keep an eye out for both positive and negative responses. Additionally, listening actively to others demonstrates a degree of respect that can serve as the cornerstone of a happy partnership. To show that you've understood them, try nodding in agreement, asking questions, or repeating back key ideas to demonstrate that you're actively listening.

4. Communicate clearly

Emotional intelligence requires effective communication. Having the right words to say the right things at the right times is essential for building strong relationships. For instance, in order to keep everyone in the workplace informed, managers must communicate objectives and goals. Make an effort to communicate with others as much as you can and provide them with a variety of ways to express their emotions to you.

5. Stay positive

Individuals with emotional intelligence are aware of the impact that a nice word, supportive email, or thoughtful gesture may have. When you can keep your cool under pressure, you can also help those around you to do the same. This mindset can also promote more cooperation and problem-solving. Even if experiencing unpleasant emotions can be acceptable, think about creating plans to lessen their impact and search for answers.

6. Show compassion

Being able to put yourself in another person's shoes is a key component of emotional intelligence. It shows that you can put yourself in someone else's shoes and respond thoughtfully and comfortingly to their feelings, even if you're not going through them yourself. Imagine yourself in another person's position to have a feel for the emotions you could experience if you were in their shoes.

7. Be receptive

Because of their empathetic nature and ability to listen attentively, those with a developed emotional intelligence tend to be more sociable. Additionally, they're open to new ideas and eager to learn. If you're stuck on a problem and can't think of a solution, try to imagine how you may apply a fresh idea to your regular tasks.

8. Listen to feedback

Being able to absorb and internalize feedback is key, whether it's praise for a recent presentation or more constructive criticism on how to distribute tasks more efficiently. You can tell you're ready to improve yourself and take responsibility for your behavior by how you handle criticism. Try to see criticism as an opportunity for growth, even though it may be painful to hear at times.

9. Remain calm when under pressure

The ability to remain calm and optimistic in the face of adversity is crucial. Working under pressure makes people anxious, so it helps if everyone can keep their cool and focus on solving the problem. Develop strategies to deal with stressful situations, including practicing deep breathing or reaching out for assistance, so you can keep your cool and composure.

Exercise: Developing Emotional Intelligence

Description: This exercise focuses on enhancing your emotional intelligence, allowing you to explore and understand your emotions more effectively. Developing emotional intelligence contributes to better self-awareness and improved interpersonal relationships.

Instructions:

- Emotion Journaling: Create a dedicated section in your workbook for emotions. Regularly journal your emotions, describing their intensity and the situations triggering them.
- Identifying Triggers: Analyze your emotion journal to identify common triggers. Note patterns and recurring themes that influence your emotional responses.
- Mindfulness Meditation: Include a mindfulness meditation practice in your daily schedule. Use guided mindfulness exercises to observe your emotions without judgment. This practice enhances your ability to respond rather than react.
- Empathy Building: Practice empathetic listening in your interactions with others. Focus on understanding their perspectives and emotions. Record your experiences and insights in your workbook.

- Emotion Regulation Techniques: Learn and record the results of many methods for controlling your emotions, such as progressive muscle relaxation, visualization, and deep breathing. Learn to adapt your strategies based on your unique needs.

- Conflict Resolution Simulation: Role-play a conflict resolution scenario. Make use of your enhanced emotional intelligence to handle the situation with understanding, clear expression of ideas, and an eye toward finding a solution.

- Continuous Learning: Continue to educate yourself on the topic of emotional intelligence. Read books, attend workshops, or listen to podcasts that deepen your understanding of emotions and their impact on well-being.

- Integration Reflection: Reflect on how the development of emotional intelligence has influenced your relationships, self-perception, and overall emotional well-being. Keep track of specific instances where enhanced emotional intelligence led to positive outcomes.

Reparenting the inner child and defining the ideal self

The brain is particularly responsive up until the age of 4. This implies that the knowledge we use moving forward and our emotional routines will be greatly influenced by the experiences we've had up to that moment. Our brains developed our unique survival strategies based on the roles (verbal or nonverbal) that we were expected to perform in our families. These strategies were developed by studying how the adults in our lives dealt with different emotions, especially grief and anger. When it comes to making decisions, the unconscious mind uses this as a kind of script. Examining and rewriting that script is possible when you nurture and reparent your inner child. How, then, would you go about achieving that?

Formulate a dialogue

In order to care for and heal your inner child, you must first recognize that it exists. Say something basic like "I see you", or "I hear you" at first, and when you're ready to go a little farther, take the time to actually get to know them. Using journaling, therapy, or meditation, sit down and set out to establish a connection with your inner child. Tell them you want to make decisions that are in their best interests right now and that you respect their consent and safety. Your inner child must understand they can break out from this never-ending loop of the past, but safety and trust must first be built before that can happen.

This can serve as a template for future conversations you have with your inner child. Remind yourself to check in with them, return later, and pay attention to their needs.

Examine or recreate photos

Look at old pictures of yourself if you have them to help you reconnect with any emotional scripts you might need to rewrite. If you were neglected, you might want to cuddle up with yourself and offer gentle affirmations of love and safety as you gaze at those photos.

Give them room to play

Play is an essential component of development; it helps kids learn and grow. Finding your inner child may require you to play, alone or with your friends, in areas where you weren't given enough room to do so. As we become older, we tend to devaluate play, dismissing it as something too juvenile for responsible adults to partake in. However, that couldn't be farther from the truth — play can heal.

Did you ever want a game or toy as a kid that you were forbidden from having? Maybe a trampoline, an easy bake oven, or a day at the park. Invest in that experience for your inner child, if that is possible. Provide purely recreational possibilities.

Say affirmations out loud to your inner child

Put some healing affirmations on a sticky note in your room and jot down the ones that your inner child would want to hear. Take a few moments each morning to read these positive affirmations out loud to your inner child.

To kick things off, here are a few suggestions:

- "I love you."
- "I apologize for what we went through."
- "You are entitled to bodily autonomy."
- "You are entitled to play and explore."
- "Your body is a good place to be."

Exercise: Reparenting and Defining Ideal Self

Description: This exercise is centered around reparenting your inner child and creating a clear vision of your ideal self. By providing the care and guidance your inner child needs, you pave the way for personal growth and the manifestation of your authentic self.

Instructions:

- Defining Ideal Self: Envision your ideal self in various aspects of life – emotionally, mentally, physically, and socially. Create a detailed description of this ideal self in your workbook.

- Identifying Parental Messages: Reflect on messages or beliefs instilled by your caregivers during your childhood. Evaluate whether these messages align with your ideal self. Note any discrepancies.

- Reparenting Visualization: Close your eyes and visualize yourself as the nurturing parent your inner child needs. Imagine providing comfort, guidance, and unconditional love. Visualize your inner child feeling safe and accepted. Write a letter from the perspective of the inner child to your present expressing its needs and the support it would like. This helps you better understand who you are now.

- Parental Affirmations: Develop affirmations that align with the nurturing messages you want to internalize. These affirmations should reinforce your ideal self and counteract any negative beliefs from your past.

- Integration Practice: Incorporate reparenting practices into your daily routine. This could involve self-care rituals, positive self-talk, and intentional actions that align with your ideal self.

- Creating a Vision Board: Use a vision board to create a picture of your ideal self. Include images and words that resonate with the qualities and aspirations of your ideal self.

CHAPTER EIGHT

KEEPING YOUR INNER CHILD ALIVE

What is humanity's greatest gift? Our creative imagination.

We can go anywhere and do anything with this gift. We made excellent use of this gift and didn't question its effectiveness until we were 4 or 5 years old. We used it to create vivid mental images of the activities and locations we desired to experience. We even imagined ourselves possessing superhuman abilities like flying or leaping between the roofs of buildings.

However, as soon as we went to school, everything began to change. Teachers and other caring adults then began to chastise us whenever we used our imaginations. They called it daydreaming or fidgeting with one's thoughts.

We, therefore, stopped daydreaming and turned our attention to the real world, which included taking care of our siblings and academics. And when we entered adolescence and early adulthood, we began to employ our imagination in very different ways than when we fantasized about the things we wanted. We began to visualize our worst thoughts and anxieties.

An ironic thing about human beings
When we're younger, we find adult lives fascinating, but as we become older, we wish we could escape the complexities and return to our childhood.

Even though both are irrational thoughts, you can rediscover your inner child, no matter your age. And once you do, you can create an image of the life you want to lead in your head by using your imagination to filter out what is happening in your life right now.

When you were younger, you probably also had less self-judgment in addition to having a vivid imagination. And that combination is quite strong. Children aren't very aware of their limitations.

You don't need to change much as an adult, which is great news. All you need to do is remember to always listen to your inner child.

Keeping your inner child alive

To help you out and make you happier, here are a few ideas on how to be more playful and serene in your life.

1. Learn to be inquisitive and ask more fruitful questions

The key, as Albert Einstein put it, "is not to stop questioning." Curiosity has a purpose of its own. Children are inherently inquisitive, quick learners, and self-expanding revealing more of who they are. Due to a lack of prior knowledge, they learn by exploring their environment, pushing themselves to their limits, and asking questions.

Quit being so sure you know everything there is to know and start asking new, interesting questions instead. Those are ancient, recurring thoughts that cross your mind every day.

Increase your exploration and openness to new ideas. Come up with new thoughts just like a kid. Additionally, ask questions that will spark concepts and take you toward new directions. Make it your goal to gain new knowledge each day.

2. Play pretend

When you're depressed, act cheerfully. Pretend you are the prosperous, successful, loving, giving person you always wanted to be. Alternatively, imagine that your heart is radiant and connected to everyone else's.

Try to find new ways to incorporate your creativity into your routine.

3. Take more risks

Children are quite daring since they are not constrained by rules. They take a lot of risks and are fearless. Children run fast, jump off things, and engage in conversation with whomever they find interesting. Either life is a bold adventure, or it becomes nothing at all. Taking chances and being adventurous will lead to many of life's best lessons and most enjoyable experiences.

If you don't take a chance, you might be able to avoid failing, pain, and grief, but you won't be able to grow, learn, feel, love, or fully live. Thus, make new friends, start a business, and pursue the life you truly desire. You can never be sure where something might end up.

4. Stop stressing about what other people may say

A child will fully immerse themselves in everything they find appealing. They're indifferent to the opinions of others. When the right spirit moves them, they burst into singing and dancing. We worry about appearing silly as grownups. Who gives a damn?

Take the cue from your inner child and dance as if no one else is around. Sometimes, it's good to let go and do the things that encourage you to get out of bed in the morning, make you angry, or both scare and thrill you.

5. Develop your creativity

For the most part, kids don't know what's supposed to be done. They invent things, developing their own unique perspectives on and approaches to the world. This flexibility inspires fresh ideas, imaginative outlets, and exquisitely expressive works of art.

Every young person is an artist. What kind of artwork would your inner child create right now? Schedule some time each week to engage in creative endeavors. Your proficiency is irrelevant. The key is to consistently uncover new creative outlets that you never thought would make you happy or to revitalize your creativity.

Take hints from your younger self

It's possible that when you were a small child, your parents or school discouraged you from pursuing your dreams or your creative side by telling you that you couldn't. Or perhaps they stated you would never be the person you wanted to be — a lawyer, a singer, a business owner, etc.

Because you were naive, you followed their instructions and trusted their advice. You have also learned to let go of your dreams. The creative energy of the universe is and has always been inextricably linked with you. It flows through you and allowing it to flow will have amazing effects on your life.

You see, your Spirit is flawless, and it marvelously gives you directions at all times. It doesn't make mistakes. Recognize that the intense will to communicate or create anything is a sign of spiritual, unexpressed happiness. Something within you yearns to develop. You may choose to allow your imagination to go wild and nurture an exciting thought when it strikes you, or you can ignore it and be paralyzed by fear. The secret is to trust in your inherent perfection.

Never believe or declare that you're too old to do anything. At the age of 40, I still set myself new, challenging goals. I enjoy learning new things and doing things I've never done before, much as I did as a kid.

As we get older, we often allow security, dullness, and complacency to creep in. However, children don't. Children are natural actors because of their innate ability to resist boredom. They have the power to transform even the most mundane tasks into thrilling escapades. They breathe vitality into the ordinary.

Act a little and learn from your past self. Create a mental image of your best life. After that, behave as the person you wish to be. What happens will amaze and pleasure you like a child.

How to improve your self-esteem for better mental health

Emotional wellness is supported by self-esteem in several ways. An individual's self-esteem is their subjective evaluation of their value, abilities, characteristics, and worth. Self-esteem is very personal and influenced by a person's background, culture, age, and even stage of life.

There are some enduring broad trends. Many people experience a decline in their self-esteem during adolescence, which is followed by an improvement and stabilization during young adulthood and mid-life when an individual's accomplishments, skills, and sense of self become more apparent.

However, factors like health issues, which may hinder one's capacity for independence, and job status changes, which may result in a decline in income and financial security, have been connected to a decline in one's self-esteem later in life. It may influence one's emotional well-being, which in turn has an impact on their behavior in different settings. What are some strategies to raise your self-esteem in order to improve your general emotional well-being if you're feeling down about yourself? These ten suggestions might be useful.

1. Surround yourself with people who encourage you

While how you view and speak to yourself is ultimately what determines your level of self-esteem, you may change or improve how you see yourself by surrounding yourself with positive messages and positive role models.

Research has indicated that social circles play a significant role in the perpetuation of both positive and negative habits. It might be beneficial to build relationships with people who support you in pursuing your interests and skills and who have an attitude of growth, as opposed to a stagnant one. Make a conscious effort to develop rewarding and encouraging relationships with the people in your life. Studies show that social support plays a critical role in promoting self-esteem.

2. Seek validation internally rather than externally

It's normal to look for outside validation, and depending on the source, even beneficial, but it's also necessary to look within for self-validation. It's possible to begin cultivating the positive self-talk that leads to an increase in self-esteem by taking the time to reflect on and evaluate your positive traits and skills. Think back on your successes, principles, and strong points. Accept and value your originality and the qualities that make you special.

One "I'm really good at…" statement can be your starting point, and you can expand from there. Prioritize your strengths over your shortcomings or perceived shortcomings. By promoting a sense of competence and self-worth, recognizing, and appreciating your abilities can help you feel more confident about yourself.

3. Put an end to your negative self-talk

It's equally critical to stop talking badly to yourself. A vicious cycle of self-blame can easily ensue when something doesn't go according to plan. It can help you to put progress ahead of perfection if you can identify when you are thinking in this way and then correct the internal conversation.

However, negative self-talk does not always involve blaming oneself for certain faults or traits. It may also refer to your belief in your own ability to accomplish your desired outcomes or whether something is even achievable.

According to research, positive self-talk has been linked to increased emotional health and self-esteem. If you find yourself saying, "I can't do this," try replacing it with, "I can do this; I just need more time."

4. Establish realistic goals

When you set and achieve goals, you can see your capacities growing, which can help you build self-esteem. Setting goals that are both realistic and attainable —that is, ones that are, based on research, somewhat challenging to achieve but not insurmountable — is crucial.

According to research, creating and achieving S.M.A.R.T. goals — which stand for specified, measurable, achievable, realistic, and time-based — is associated with higher levels of well-being and self-worth.

It's critical to never forget to acknowledge and appreciate your small (as well as big) victories along the journey. By celebrating your victories, you can accumulate a record of accomplishments that you can refer to and recognize when engaging in constructive self-talk.

5. Exercise self-compassion

It's crucial to learn how to treat yourself with kindness and compassion when things in life don't go as planned because not every day or every circumstance will result in a victory, so to speak. You are being kind to yourself when you practice self-compassion. We often treat ourselves considerably worse than we do other people. Less overthinking, more open-mindedness and less comparison to others are all possible outcomes of self-compassion.

After a setback, practicing self-compassion increases your likelihood of eventually getting back on the horse and trying again. According to the study, people who engaged in self-compassion exercises after failing a test were more likely to study harder in preparation for a subsequent exam, which raised their chances of passing it.

6. Adopt an active lifestyle

You don't need to be an athlete or an extreme fitness enthusiast to benefit from regular exercise. Regular physical activity, even simply a 30-minute walk most days of the week, can boost self-esteem. Regular exercise has been confirmed to lessen anxiety and stress while also improving mood and self-esteem.

7. Get enough sleep

Beneficial habits that improve general health and self-care can almost always have a beneficial effect on self-esteem. Making sure you're getting enough sleep is a guaranteed method to improve your general feeling of well-being. Increasing sleep quality can boost mood and cognitive performance, which can raise self-esteem. It can also lessen irritation and increase energy.

Research has shown a strong correlation between optimism, self-esteem, and the length and quality of one's sleep. Individuals who consistently slept for seven to eight hours per night in a high-quality manner showed better levels of optimism and self-esteem than those who slept for fewer than six hours or more than nine hours.

8. Acquire new skills

Your self-esteem can be raised by personal development that increases your confidence in your skills for your job, relationships, and home life. Developing new skills can improve one's sense of accomplishment and competence and in turn, raise self-esteem. This fosters a sense of fulfillment and success.

According to a study, older people who took a 20-hour computer and technology course had a higher chance of feeling more confident about their technological skills and seeing increases in their self-esteem.

Similarly, another research study discovered that senior citizens who committed to studying a foreign language gained several advantages, such as enhanced self-worth, enhanced cognitive skills, and increased chances for social engagement.

9. Make room in your schedule for enjoyment

Doing what makes you happy will boost your self-esteem, no matter how obvious it may sound. Fun activities have been demonstrated to be a powerful means of improving mental well-being in general, which in turn increases feelings of value and self-worth.

Thus, keep in mind that scheduling time for your favorite hobbies — whether it's baking, dancing, or painting — is crucial for maintaining your mental health.

10. Consider speaking with a therapist

The events and encounters you have throughout your life, especially in the family and cultural context of your upbringing, have an impact on your sense of self-worth.

Examining prior trauma and self-esteem harm might be beneficial. Examining its origins and potential solutions can be facilitated by consulting a mental health professional.

Exercise: Dear future me

Your future self has so many bright prospects. When you think of your future, you should be excited. However, many people think of the future with fear. They worry about all the things that could go wrong. While it's true that things can and will go wrong, it's not good to linger on those things. There's no power in what you cannot control. As a result, inner child work teaches you to focus on your mastery over yourself and your ability to look within to cope with the unknowns and difficult truths.

Write a journal entry detailing what you want your future self to have. Consider what your future life will look like. Don't be afraid to be ambitious. Being a dreamer allows you to get more out of life.

_____

_____

_____

_____

_____

_____

_____

_____

_____

_____

_____

_____

_____

_____

CONCLUSION

Congratulations on reaching the end of this healing journey. You made the brave decision to embrace your inner child, face your past, and develop self-compassion and self-love. This is no small feat, so you should be proud of yourself.

As you complete this book, take a moment to reflect on all that you managed to achieve. You've looked into your childhood experiences, recognized and dealt with repressed feelings, and adopted regular routines to support your well-being. You've learned to identify and change negative thought patterns, faced hidden parts of yourself, and embraced self-compassion. Although difficult at times, this journey has been life-changing.

Completing this book is a big step forward in your journey, but healing is a lifelong process. Continue to practice the techniques and exercises you've learned. As you proceed, remember to be nice to yourself and let your newly acquired knowledge guide your decisions. Improvement isn't always linear, and that is acceptable, too. Every small win calls for celebration.

Now, let's take some time to reflect on your entire healing process and assess the changes and progress you've achieved. This reflection will help you consolidate your experiences and set intentions for your ongoing growth.

Reflecting on the healing journey

Locate a calm, cozy area where you may relax and focus. Breathe deeply a few times, and calm your thoughts. Reflect on the journey you've undertaken with this workbook, and use the space below to capture your thoughts and feelings.

Memorable moments. Reflect on the most significant moments of your journey. What memories stand out to you? Describe these moments and why they are meaningful.

_____

_____

_____

_____

Overcoming challenges. Think about the challenges you faced along the way. How did you get past them? What self-discoveries did you make during the process?

_____

_____

_____

_____

Personal growth. Consider how you've grown and changed. How has your understanding of your inner child evolved? What new strengths have you discovered?

_____

_____

_____

_____

Gratitude and appreciation. Write about the blessings you have received from this adventure. What or who has helped you? What improvements are you appreciative of?

_____

_____

_____

_____

Evaluating changes and achieving progress

Reflect on the following questions to evaluate the changes and progress you've made. Take your time to answer them thoughtfully and honestly.

How have my emotions changed?

Reflect on your emotional state before you began this workbook and compare it to how you feel now. What changes do you notice in your emotional well-being?

_____

_____

_____

_____

What new insights have I gained?

Consider the new insights you've gained about yourself, your inner child, and your past. How have they impacted your perspective and behavior?

_____

_____

_____

_____

What positive changes have I made in my daily life?

Think about the self-care practices and techniques you've incorporated into your daily routine. How have these changes improved your overall well-being?

_____

_____

_____

_____

How have my relationships improved?

Reflect on any changes in your relationships with others. What effects has your journey had on the relationships and interactions you have with loved ones, family, and friends?

_____

_____

_____

_____

What goals have I achieved?

Look back at the goals you set for yourself at the beginning of this workbook. What targets have you met? When you accomplish them, how does it feel?

_____

_____

_____

_____

What challenges remain?

Acknowledge any challenges or areas of your life that still need attention. How are you going to deal with these issues going forward?

_____

_____

_____

_____

What are my next steps?

Consider the next steps in your healing journey. What actions will you take to continue your growth and maintain your progress? What new goals will you set for yourself?

_____

_____

_____

_____

Moving forward

As you go, keep in mind that healing is an ongoing process. Be kind to yourself and keep applying the techniques and strategies you have learned. No matter how small your progress may seem, acknowledge it and continue working for a happier, healthier life. You have an inner child, who is a part of you and deserves love, understanding, and compassion. If you take care of this relationship, it will keep pointing you in the direction of self-awareness and peace of mind.

Thank you for believing in yourself on this journey and for dedicating yourself to healing. Your experience is a testament to your strength and resilience. Keep shining brightly with your light, and remember that you have the ability to create a happy and beautiful future.

FROM INNER CHILD TO SHADOW WORK

Explore the Shadow Work Journal and Workbook as a natural continuation of your journey with Inner Child. Here, you will delve into the depths of your psyche, analyzing and embracing the darker aspects of yourself. Through practical exercises and thoughtful guidance, the book provides you with the necessary tools to integrate the shadow, thereby completing your personal growth journey. Take the Shadow Work book to continue illuminating every corner of your essence and embrace a comprehensive transformation.

Scan the QR-Code to get it:

EXCLUSIVE BONUSES FOR YOUR INNER CHILD JOURNEY

Welcome to the bonus page of your Inner Child book! I have prepared two special gifts for you that you can obtain by downloading the files through the link below.

BONUS #1: SHADOW WORK AND INNER CHILD HEALING AUDIOBOOKS

This exclusive audiobook guides you through the process of uncovering and healing hidden parts of yourself. Listen anytime, anywhere, and explore your shadow with ease, gaining deep insights and self-awareness.

BONUS #2: AFFIRMATIONS FOR INNER CHILD HEALING

These affirmations are a loving invitation to heal your inner child. Repeat them consistently to warmly welcome the past, creating a secure space for transformation.

BONUS #3: 5 EXTRA EXERCISES TO EXPLORE YOUR SHADOW

The second bonus that I offer is a series of guided and additional exercises to the books on shadow work. These exercises will help you deepen your work on the shadow and further develop your self-awareness.

I am excited to offer these bonuses to my readers and hope that they will help you further progress in your inner child journey. Do not hesitate to download the files through the link below to access the bonuses and start exploring your inner self right away!

Your support is important to me!

Great things can start from a small gesture!

Leave a sincere review to support my work.

This would help to share and find this knowledge more easily for people

who are looking for it.

REFERENCES

Ackerman, C. E., MA. (2023, September 20). *Cognitive restructuring techniques for reframing thoughts*. PositivePsychology.com. https://positivepsychology.com/cbt-cognitive-restructuring-cognitive-distortions/

Buchwald, N. (2023a, June 15). *Embracing Inner Child Work: Reparent and heal your inner child*. Manhattan Mental Health Counseling. https://manhattanmentalhealthcounseling.com/embracing-inner-child-work-reparent-and-heal-your-inner-child/

Buchwald, N. (2023b, June 15). *Embracing Inner Child Work: Reparent and heal your inner child*. Manhattan Mental Health Counseling. https://manhattanmentalhealthcounseling.com/embracing-inner-child-work-reparent-and-heal-your-inner-child

Choosing Therapy. (2023, December 28). *8 tips for healing your inner Child*. https://www.choosingtherapy.com/inner-child-healing/

Gillihan, S., PhD. (2023, May 31). *10 ways to boost your emotional health*. EverydayHealth.com. https://www.everydayhealth.com/emotional-health/10-ways-to-boost-emotional-health.aspx

Goldstein, E. (2021, August 28). *Accessing your Inner Child : A Step Toward Healing — Integrative Psychotherapy Mental Health blog*. https://integrativepsych.co/new-blog/inner-child-work-exercise

Good, S. &qout;. (2023, October 7). *How to keep your inner child alive*. Honey Good®. https://www.honeygood.com/how-to-keep-your-inner-child-alive/

Hopeful Panda. (2023, November 17). *Inner Child Work: 10 Ways to Connect with Your Inner Child*. https://hopefulpanda.com/inner-child/

Lim, E. (2022, January 4). How to Reparent Yourself: A starter guide for inner child healing. *Medium*. https://medium.com/wholistique/how-to-reparent-yourself-a-starter-guide-for-inner-child-healing-398cc0d7fa28

Mfa, R. J. S. (2023, June 5). *How to Change Negative Thinking with Cognitive Restructuring*. Healthline. https://www.healthline.com/health/cognitive-restructuring#fa-qs

Rusnak, A. (2023, January 23). *8 ways to accept your past and move forward*. Ann Rusnak - AR Success | From Stuck to Unstoppable Success. https://annrusnak.com/8-ways-to-accept-your-past-and-move-forward/

Trauma-Informed CBT for adults: What is it & how it helps. (2021, July 14). https://www.encomiumpsychology.com/trauma-informed-cbt-adults

User, S. (n.d.). *Setting Boundaries with Inner Children | Book Content*. https://www.healyourinnerchild.com/book-content/setting-boundaries-with-inner-children

Zoella, T. (2022, February 22). *How to Connect with Your Inner Child to Heal, Evolve & Blossom in Adulthood - Zoella*. Zoella. https://www.zoella.co.uk/2022/02/22/how-to-connect-with-your-inner-child-to-heal-evolve-blossom-in-adulthood/

Made in United States
Troutdale, OR
03/22/2025